SECOND EDITION
PURE GOLD

HOW I BUILT A $37 MILLION INSURANCE AGENCY IN LESS THAN 7 YEARS

DARREN SUGIYAMA

Title:
How I Built A $37 Million Insurance Agency In Less Than 7 Years

Copyright © 2020 Darren Sugiyama
All rights reserved.

ISBN: 978-0-9892619-4-4

CONTENTS

Foreword: Ten Years Wiser 5

Chapter 1: Ultimate Clarity 23

Chapter 2: My First Year In The Insurance Business 31

Chapter 3: Becoming A Master Recruiter 45

Chapter 4: People-Driven vs. System-Driven 67

Chapter 5: Why Everyone Hates Scripts 81

Chapter 6: Presenting vs. Creating an Experience 95

Chapter 7: Consistency of Content 115

Chapter 8: Go F*** Yourself 127

Chapter 9: 1099 Independent Contractors 145

Chapter 10: New Perspective 165

Chapter 11: The Reinvention of The DSCs 191

About The Author 221

DARREN SUGIYAMA

FORWARD
TEN YEARS WISER

I wrote the original *First Edition* of this book in 2010 – ten years ago – and though I was successful by most people's standards, I only now realize just how naïve and full of ego I was back then.

Have you ever heard the question, "What would you tell your 10-years younger self if you could go back in time?"

For me, the list of things I wish I would have known when I first started my insurance agency seventeen years ago is almost infinite. This knowledge would have drastically shortened my learning curve and saved me from having to reinvent the wheel.

But even within the last ten years, I have learned a completely new set of invaluable lessons – lessons I believe are even more valuable than the ones I wrote about in the *First Edition*, hence the impetus to write the *Second Edition* of this book.

Though the struggle of having to develop a business model from ground zero certainly builds character and resilience, often times it is difficult to find clarity in the midst of uncertainty.

One of the most painful lessons I've learned over the last ten years is that the people you start out with are not necessarily the people you finish with.

I've lost many faux-friends and agents over the years, but these relationships have been replaced by much better ones.

There is definitely a higher-caliber of person I do business with today versus ten years ago. In fact, even within the last three years, the quality of people I do business with has exponentially improved.

I am also certain that these higher-caliber people I am partnered with today would not have partnered with me if I was still associated with many of these people from the past.

As much as I tried to drag some of those people of the past across the finish line with me, I have learned that sometimes you have to stop watering dead plants and gracefully let them move on, and sometimes you have to make the decision to move on without them.

Sometimes you have to cut out the cancer.

And sometimes, God does it for you.

I've gone through several massive betrayals – both in business relationships and personal relationships – and when you experience this more than a few times, it is natural to question yourself.

If you have experienced something similar to this, you probably obsessed over what happened, agonizing over why these relationships dissolved. You want answers.

Well, perhaps God heard conversations that you did not.

Perhaps this was a necessary *pruning*.

Pruning is not a loss, but rather a necessary extrication of certain people from your life for your own protection, well-being and future success.

These people probably did you a favor by leaving.

It may not feel like it right now, but over time – and I speak from personal experience on this one – you will find that it would have been impossible to succeed at the level you were destined for if those people were still in your life.

You may not have this ultimate clarity at the moment.

I certainly didn't have clarity or peace of mind back when I went through these betrayals.

But I have it now and want you to have it too.

In this book, I will share with you how I got through many of these awful experiences, and how my business is in a much better position today. I'll also share with you why I'm enjoying my work now more than ever before.

Sure, recalibrating and improving your business model affords you the opportunity to make a lot more money, but revenue generation only constitutes for one of several elements that make a great business *great*.

Being ten years older, ten years wiser, and a whole lot more mature than I was when I wrote the *First Edition* of this book, there are lessons – life changing lessons – that I would love to be able to share with my gun-slinging, ego-driven, 10-years younger self.

But since hopping in Doc's *DeLorean* and time-traveling back to 2010 like Marty McFly to teach my 38-year old self is not possible, my 48-year old self has decided to teach you everything I did right… everything I did wrong… everything I would have done differently… and everything I'm doing now.

This is the purpose of me writing this *Second Edition*.

Seventeen years has gone by so fast, and the last ten years even faster. When I wrote the *First Edition*, I really thought I had mastered the game. I was flying around the country giving motivational talks and doing insurance sales coaching for thousands of agents. I have even been referred to as *The Tony Robbins Of The Insurance Industry*.

But at the height of success in my first insurance agency, which was just a few years after I wrote the *First Edition*, I decided to completely change directions.

One could argue that these moves were unnecessary, for I had already built a pretty successful agency doing over $37 million in annual premium.

Why on earth would I attempt to do something new when I was already one of the most notorious figures in the employee benefits industry?

The reason was that deep down in my gut, I felt like there was something missing.

The Metamorphosis

The year after I published the *First Edition* of this book, I launched a voluntary benefits agency with my wife called *Pacific Bay Insurance Group*.

Two years later, I launched a life insurance agency called *DaVinci Financial* that started off selling life insurance policies to business owners over the phone, and later evolved into offering retirement solutions to employees of companies at their worksite.

A few years later, I launched a firm that specialized in premium financing – the most sophisticated niche within the life insurance industry. Many people have tried to make it in this high-end niche and failed, for there are only a handful of players in this space who have all the market share.

Squeezing my way into this already-crowded space seemed impossible to many.

Similar to Noah announcing he was going to build an arc, it was difficult getting people on board with me in the beginning. After years of going through several of the *wrong* business partners, I finally found the *right* business partner.

That's when everything changed for me.

Partnering with the *right* person – whether in business or in a marriage – can either ruin your life, or make you soar.

I have been blessed to have found the right business partner and the right wife, and the combination of each of these two *different-but-similar* relationships has greatly contributed to me soaring.

Lionsmark Capital – our premium financing firm – has accomplished quite a bit in a relatively short amount of time.

I must admit, our aspirations in the beginning certainly seemed delusional to the outside eye, but I believe that if your aspirations sound reasonable, then they're not big enough.

There is a fine line between delusion and genius.

Earlier this year, I had one very successful gentleman in the financial services industry ask me, "What made you think you could jump in and immediately compete with the biggest players in the premium financing industry that have owned this space for over 20 years?"

I replied, "Well, you've been in this space for over 20 years, and you've stopped doing business with my competitors, and now you're doing business with me. Why is that?"

He smiled and responded, "Because you guys have developed something superior. Your stuff is just better than everyone else's."

Every industry *Goliath* was once a delusional *David*.

Though we've been doing premium financing for several years at the retail level, we're now in our third official year as an intermediary firm.

Currently, almost all of our cases are brought to us by carriers, IMOs, investment firms, and agents who used to be our competitors, but have now become our partners.

In less than three years of entering this intermediary space, we have established ourselves as one of the most dominant players in the entire premium financing industry.

We have secured our position as one of the most trusted premium financing intermediaries by over a dozen life insurance carriers, and we have established proprietary lending relationships with banks that none of our competitors have access to.

We've used our strategy with individual clients whose net worth ranges from $20 million to $1.2 billion, as well as inside an endowment for a private university.

So the question is, *How did I do it?*

It was not an easy transition by any means.

But what allowed me to make these seemingly impossible moves came down to a few simple variables that needed to align.

1. I was able to identify a void in a multi-billion dollar industry.
2. I figured out how I could fill that void in way that had never been done before.
3. I aligned myself with the right business partner.

Once I was able to get each of these three variables aligned – especially the third one – I had ultimate clarity in regards to my first step into these unchartered waters.

In business, *clarity* answers two very important questions:

1. What exactly should I do right now?
2. How exactly should I do it?

In this book, I will help you discover the answers to these two important questions as it pertains to building your insurance agency, and I will share with you how I have reinvented myself in great detail.

Love Thy Haters

Over the last ten years, the *First Edition* of this book has been one of the top ranking insurance-related books on *Amazon*.

But the *First Edition* of this book was written by my 10-years younger self.

Back then I was still *green*, and it was also the first book I had ever written. As I re-read it during the rewrite of this *Second Edition*, it made me realize just how much has changed since then, not only in my business model, but also in my understanding of who I am, who I want to be, and who I no longer want to be.

As part of my process in writing this *Second Edition*, I also decided to scour the internet, reading every single review that I could find on the *First Edition* – both positive and negative. Reading online reviews is a slippery slope, because often times you may read things you don't want to read, and see things you don't want to see.

As much positive feedback as I've gotten on several of my books (this is my seventh published book), I've also read some very negative reviews posted online about my work.

It reminds me of *Mean Tweets* – the segment on the TV show *Jimmy Kimmel Live!* – wherein celebrities read awful comments posted about them on *Twitter*.

The entire segment is hilarious, because it is further proof that no matter how successful and famous a person becomes, there are still people that feel the need to say bad things about them.

For the most part, these celebrities have a really good sense of humor about these terrible things said about them.

Watching them laugh at these *tweets* actually helped me develop a sense of humor about the things my haters have posted about me.

Here are just a few of the negative *Amazon* reviews of the *First Edition* of this book for your entertainment.

★☆☆☆☆ **This book is BS**
By R. Alberson II on November 17, 2014
Format: Hardcover   Verified Purchase

Outdated information that has not applied to this industry for many years.

★★☆☆☆ **Not worth the cost of the paper**
By Steven on August 25, 2014
Format: Paperback   Verified Purchase

★☆☆☆☆ **Useless**
By GramFall4 on January 18, 2015
Format: Paperback   Verified Purchase

This book is more of an ego trip for the author and not worth the money.

★★☆☆☆ **How I built a $37 million insurance agnecy**
By drtom on August 19, 2012
Format: Hardcover   Verified Purchase

Didn't get a lot out of this. It does nothing for an independent sales person. I had a hard time reading about his struggles and living off his friends couches and such, and being broke, when at the end of the book, it talks about how he came from another high paying position at another company. Has some interesting information but I was looking for insight on how to gain more insurance clients and not manage or gain a sales force.

My favorite review is this last one.

First, because he misspelled the word *agency*, and second, because he said he had no interest in managing or gaining a sales force. Uh, the title of the book is *How I Built A $37 Million Insurance Agency*, not *How To Gain More Insurance Clients*.

What made his criticism even more shocking to me is that the *First Edition* actually did give some very specific tips on how to acquire more insurance clients – three full chapters actually – including how to book an appointment with a prospect over the phone, how to structure your product offering, how to unseat the incumbent broker, and how to close the deal.

It just goes to show, you can't please everybody.

But back to the title of the book, why would he buy a book with the title *How I Built A $37 Million Insurance Agency* if he didn't want to build an insurance agency?

That's like buying a book on how to open and run a successful restaurant, and then criticizing the book because you only wanted to learn how to make a killer ribeye steak.

To be completely transparent, in the beginning stages of my career as an author, I used to read these types of negative reviews and they would get under my skin.

Despite a few negative reviews, the reality was that 53% of the reviews gave my book a 5-Star rating, 12% gave it a 4-star rating, and 10% gave it a 3-Star rating.

So 75% of the reviews were positive, and over half of the reviews actually gave my book the highest rating possible.

But as human beings, what do we do?

We focus on the negative comments, not the positive ones.

Of course, I received far more positive reviews than negative ones, but that's not the point.

The point is, regardless of how big or small you grow your agency, you will undoubtedly encounter people that feel the need to criticize you and put you down.

No one is immune to the criticism of other people.

Haters gonna hate.

Google anyone you think is beyond reproach, and I guarantee you will find something negative posted about them. I even found an article in the *Huffington Post* that criticized Mother Teresa, saying, "She was no saint."

http://www.huffingtonpost.com/krithika-varagur/mother-teresa-was-no-saint_b_9470988.html

Now, if there are people in this world that are going to talk negatively about Mother Teresa, there are certainly people that will talk negatively about you too.

Every person that has the guts to attempt to do something extraordinary will get chastised for it. It's always been this way.

As Aristotle once said, "There is only one way to avoid criticism: *Do* nothing, *say* nothing, and *be* nothing."

If you're going to be successful in life and in business, you're going to be mercilessly criticized, but you always have to consider the source. Many of the negative things said about you probably come from people that aren't very successful, intelligent or rational.

The great Babe Ruth said, "The loudest boos always come from the cheapest seats."

In fact, do this: *Google* the names of your harshest critics, and you know what you'll find?

Nothing, because they've never accomplished anything great.

13

What helped me mentally and emotionally process this negative feedback was a famous inspirational speech given by Theodore Roosevelt. It is called *The Man In The Arena*, and is one of my favorite speeches of all time.

The Man In The Arena

It is not the critic who counts;

Not the man who points out how the strong man stumbles, or where the doer of deeds could have done them better.

The credit belongs to the man who is actually in the arena, whose face is marred by dust and sweat and blood;

Who strives valiantly, who errs, who comes short again and again, because there is no effort without error and shortcoming;

But who does actually strive to do the deeds;

Who knows great enthusiasms, the great devotions;

Who spends himself in a worthy cause;

Who at the best knows in the end the triumph of high achievement, and who at the worst, if he fails, at least fails while daring greatly, so that his place shall never be with those cold and timid souls who neither know victory nor defeat.

You will face heavy criticism as an entrepreneur, and if you have employees and 1099 agents, you will ferociously be accused of everything under the sun.

You wouldn't believe the insanely ridiculous things I've been accused of and blamed for by ex-agents and ex-employees.

Some of them are truly unbelievable.

Bitter, unsuccessful and disgruntled people will undoubtedly point the finger at someone else for their lack of success or unhappiness, and that *someone* will be you.

You must be willing to accept this.

I used to obsess about what people have posted about me and my companies on some of these websites that allow anyone to write a negative review about an employer with no fact-checking whatsoever.

Don't get overly caught up in what other people post about you online. If an agent candidate reads something negative about you online and decides not to interview with you, they are probably not very rational or intelligent anyway. Their decision to pass on your agency probably saved you from wasting your time and energy on an irrational, blame-oriented, negative person.

If you're getting some bad internet reviews and you have people posting negative things about you right now, it's probably a sign that you're pretty successful.

Don't fret. Take it as a compliment.

When I was in college, I was a 2nd Team All-Conference baseball player at *Loyola Marymount University*, leading the conference in RBIs my Junior year.

I remember playing against the *University of San Francisco* at their stadium, and they had a crew of fans parked out in left field talking trash to me the entire game.

They were all over me, saying awful things about my family, my girlfriend and me. When I went up to bat, they had a whole section of fans right behind home plate ragging me too. I wanted to beat the crap out of all of them (yes, I was a hot-head and wanted to fight everyone back then).

Afraid I was going to knock somebody out and get ejected from the game, my coach pulled me aside and told me, "Sugi, nobody boo's a benchwarmer."

This was his way of telling me that the only reason those guys were ragging me was because I was a threat to them.

I was the power hitter that was going to drive in the runs to beat them, and they knew it. Think about how much time and effort they spent researching me, prepping all the fans to rag me, plotting to try to get into my head for this series at their own home field.

All of that effort expended, focusing on me.

When I thought of it that way, it was actually a compliment.

That's the way you need to view your haters.

There is a reason they are so obsessed with you.

They are either threatened by your capabilities, or they are jealous and upset that they are not as successful as you are.

Again, take it as a compliment and love thy haters, because they will give you great insight into how to best recalibrate your process, your brand and your perspective, which I will talk about extensively in this book.

Remember, if even Mother Teresa has haters, so will you.

Why I Decided To Write The Second Edition Of This Book

I firmly believe that despite the necessity of shaking off the negative opinions that other people have of you, there is great value in seeking to understand what makes some people think and feel this way about you – even the unreasonable ones.

Don't let the their criticisms get to you, but don't ignore them either. You can learn a lot by studying them like lab rats.

There is a fine line between letting their criticisms get under your skin, versus evaluating them in the way that a clinical psychologist evaluates a mentally ill patient, or the way a CSI agent studies a crime scene looking for clues.

I have spent the last ten years of my 17-year insurance career evaluating what I've done right, what I've done wrong, and what I would change.

The *First Edition* of this book explained how I built my agency during the first seven years.

About half of the content in this *Second Edition* is identical to the *First Edition*, however I will also share with you what I've learned over the last ten years and how I've updated and recalibrated my own business practices.

I am a much different animal today – stronger, faster, and quite frankly, better. My experiences have made me more resilient and far wiser, and I now know which battles are worth fighting, and which ones are not worth fighting.

In addition, I have done quite a bit of introspective thinking, analyzing some of the criticisms of my *First Edition*. I asked myself, "Do any of these criticisms have *some* legitimate merit?"

Well, one of the criticisms said that the book was too general and didn't give enough detail regarding my *trade secrets*.

In my defense, there is only so much detail you can fit into a 100-page book, but I still took that criticism under consideration.

That's why this *Second Edition* is almost double the length of the *First Edition*, mapping out some of the specific strategies I've used, along with giving you frameworks of how to emulate these strategies in your specific line of business – whether you're in employee benefits, supplemental insurance, property and casualty, life insurance, annuities – whatever you specialize in.

Plus, I have ten additional years of experience under my belt compared to when I published the *First Edition*.

That's ten additional years of new experiences.

Ten additional years of wisdom developed.

Ten additional years to mature as a man.

Ten Years Ago vs. Today

A lot has changed in the last ten years.

Ten years ago on March 23, 2010, President Obama signed into law the *Affordable Care Act (ACA)* colloquially known as *ObamaCare*. This completely changed the employee benefits business landscape, which was my core business back then.

Technology has changed exponentially as well. In April 2010, the first generation of the *iPad* came out – a device that would change how we consume media and communicate with each other forever. Since then, *Apple* has sold more than 400 million *iPads*. It's hard to imagine that just a decade ago, the *iPad* did not exist.

Later that same year on October 6, 2010, *Instagram* launched. In the last ten years, this type of social media platform has influenced people to feel the need to post pictures that make their fake lives look cooler than their friends' fake lives. *Keeping Up*

With The Joneses is now *Keeping Up With The Kardashians*, with *self-made* billionaire Kylie Jenner leading the charge. At the time of me writing this *Second Edition*, Kylie Jenner had 175 million followers, with one of her posts – a single post – receiving 18 million *likes*.

Bruce Jenner is now *Caitlyn Jenner*. If you're wondering how this is relevant to the insurance business, my firm placed a life insurance policy on client that was genetically born a male, but transitioned to a female through full gender reassignment surgery, and the carrier issued the policy using female rates instead of male underwriting guidelines.

Bill Cosby went from being beloved as *America's Dad* to being a convicted sex offender, sentenced to prison in 2018. One year prior to Cosby's conviction, the *#metoo* movement had gone viral in 2017 spurring over 19 million tweets. The sensitivity regarding co-worker interactions in the workplace was heightened tremendously, drastically changing the workplace environment and co-worker communication dynamics.

In the last ten years, we have experienced the first African-American *President Of The United States* in the history of this country in Barack Obama. We have also experienced Donald Trump going from billionaire real estate mogul, to reality TV show icon, to our current *President Of The United States*.

In these last ten years, we've experienced the longest bull market in the history of the U.S. economy, but when COVID-19 crashed the market in March 2020, we experienced the steepest one-day fall of the stock market since the crash in 1987.

So here we are in 2020, and the Coronavirus pandemic has all of us quarantined, working remotely from our homes, with the future of *normal* business practices facing complete uncertainty.

Suffice to say, a lot has changed in the last ten years.

What Is The Future Of American Business?

The world has dramatically changed. This is our new normal.

In business, only the strong survive.

But perhaps an even more appropriate statement is that only the strong, nimble and creative survive.

Remember *Circuit City*? *Blockbuster Video*? *Tower Records*?

These were dominant companies in their space at one time.

But what happened?

For *Circuit City* and so many other retail superstores, a little online bookstore called *Amazon* came along and decided to evolve into a worldwide retail source for just about everything consumed by a human being, and the face of retail as we once knew it was changed forever.

Blockbuster Video? Hello *Netflix*. Goodbye *Blockbuster*.

Tower Records? Hello streaming services. Goodbye *Tower*.

And *Amazon*? Enter *Amazon Prime*, a subscription-based priority delivery service. Enter *Prime Video*, a subscription-based entertainment platform offering movies and music. Now you can even purchase groceries with home delivery service through *Amazon Fresh*.

Remember, there was a time when *Amazon* was merely an unprofitable online bookstore.

Amazon – and perhaps more accurately stated, the brilliant Jeff Bezos – is a *Thought Leader*.

Part of being a *Thought Leader* means that 99% of their crazy outside-the-box ideas will crash and burn, and when they do, they get heavily criticized for it – sometimes even ridiculed. They have to hear all the snickers from the peanut gallery, and the peanut gallery loves to see the *Thought Leader* fail.

Thought Leaders must accept this as part of their life.

The first one through the wall always gets the most bloody, and is also scrutinized and criticized the most.

Thought Leaders have ideas that are rejected by the masses, and initially, sometimes even by the *Early Adopters*.

If the *Thought Leader* is too far ahead of their time, even the *Early Adopters* will not buy into their crazy ideas, unless a

19

completely unforeseen tragedy strikes that destroys the old business paradigm overnight.

When the sky falls, it is the *Thought Leaders* who are already in position to capture huge market share because they already have the infrastructure and track record to prove that a necessary alternative approach to conducting business can be successfully executed.

The *Laggards* will sulk and bury their heads in the sand.

The *Early Adopters* will quickly pivot and learn from the *Thought Leaders*, benefiting the most from the *Thought Leader*'s crazy ideas.

The *Thought Leader* instantly gains bragging rights.

But the fair market value of bragging rights isn't going to buy a *Thought Leader* a new jet or a private island in the Caribbean.

Forget bragging rights and the ego gratification of telling all of your haters "I told you so."

The real opportunity for the *Thought Leader* is to build a small team of intelligent, highly skilled *Early Adopters*, and execute what the mere mortals in their industry cannot fathom doing.

Back in 2010, just after I wrote the *First Edition* of this book, I started experimenting with virtual selling – selling employee benefits completely over the phone – where my agents would never have to leave the office.

As always, everyone told me it wouldn't work.

So what did I do?

I used myself as the guinea pig. I built a *PowerPoint* presentation and a script to go along with it. I used a screenshare program, and did my entire business owner meetings virtually from my office, completely over the phone and screenshare.

I initially got dismal results.

But just like my unorthodox approach in the very beginning of my insurance career, I just needed to tweak it and tune it just right to hit the perfect sweet spot.

Once I got it there, I knew I was on to something big.

I reviewed it with my two top agents, and we ran a parallel pilot test. Both agents being of comparable skill, one agent continued run meetings face-to-face. The other, 100% phone-based meetings, screensharing my *PowerPoint* presentation, reading from my script.

After three months, the face-to-face agent had closed 29 new group health insurance clients. Yes, I trained him well.

The other agent never left the office. He did everything over the phone and screenshare, and in that same period of time, he closed 31 new group health insurance clients. Yes, I trained him well too.

I identified several benefits of virtual-selling over the phone:

1. Quality Control. I could sit shotgun with a new agent to see exactly what they were saying, and even silently coach them through the call in real time.

2. Higher Density of Appointments. No drive time meant more phone time. The most face-to-face meetings an agent could run in a day was only 3-4 (depending on how far apart each appointment was from each other), whereas my agents could run 7-8 appointments a day over the phone due to zero drive time.

3. Expansion of Territory. Instead of being geographically limited to a reasonable driving radius from our office, we could transact business with no geographic restrictions.

I thought that the sheer increase in our volume of appointments would make up for any decrease in closing percentage that the less-personal interaction of a virtual screenshare meeting would result in.

Yes, the volume of appointments increased, but to my pleasant surprise, that's not all that increased.

The virtual-style employer meetings actually *increased* our closing percentage from 24% to 31%.

I took what I learned in developing this virtual model in the employee benefits space, and started a completely separate life insurance agency called *DaVinci Financial*.

DaVinci started cold-calling into 17 different states.

We did the entire process over the phone, including taking the application, scheduling the paramed, and delivering the policy – all virtually, never meeting the client in-person.

The fact that we could now do business out of state from the comfort of our main office in Irvine, California meant I could get six additional hours of production per day – three more hours in the morning calling the East Coast, and three more hours in the evening calling into Hawaii – which meant almost double the revenue-generating hours in a workday.

We had out-of-state life insurance clients sending $10,000 to $400,000 annual premium checks to an agency they're never heard of, trusting an agent they've never met in-person.

This was all done virtually, over the phone.

Basically, I built a virtual selling model in the insurance world a full decade before the Coronavirus pandemic ever forced us to sell over the phone.

A *Thought Leader* innovates before he is forced to innovate.

A *Thought Leader* accepts being criticized for attempting to fix what ain't broke, anticipating that his innovation will one day make him a legend.

Good is unacceptable.

Great is never enough.

For a true *Thought Leader,* the only acceptable outcome is to become *legendary*.

Whatever type of insurance you specialize in, the old conventional way of transacting business might not be the *only* way it can be done.

Sometimes, *impossible* works better.

CHAPTER 1

ULTIMATE CLARITY

I Am A Clarifier

There are so many different types of people that I've worked with over the years.

Some of them have been extremely driven and some have been extremely lazy. Some have a do-whatever-it-takes attitude, and some have an excuse for everything. Some have been people of their word, and some live their lives based on situational ethics.

One thing I've found in my business life – as well as in my personal life – is that there are some things you can teach people and some things you cannot.

Integrity, honesty, character, work ethic and humility are things of the heart, and things of the heart cannot be taught. These valuable qualities are just part of that person's DNA.

Believe me, I've tried to change people – attempting to motivate them to be more ambitious, more driven, more honest – and I have failed miserably each and every time.

That's one of the biggest misconceptions about great leaders.

A great leader doesn't seek to *change* people.

A great leader doesn't try to *motivate* people.

A great leader doesn't attempt to *convince* people to change their ways.

In my opinion, the definition of a great leader is one who helps people *clarify* what their actual goals are.

A great leader gives their disciples step-by-step, systematic directives on how to both identify and accomplish their goals, not convince them what their goals *should* be.

I'm not a motivator.

I'm a clarifier.

My job is to provide ultimate clarity to my people.

For my clients, I provide the kind of clarity that makes it easy for them to pull the trigger without hesitation or reservation. My entire goal is to give them such a unique experience – an experience that provides such clarity – that they cannot come up with a reason to not do business with me.

I will often times literally tell them, "By the end of this conversation, you are going to run out of reasons to not do this."

When I do this, everyone wins, especially my clients.

When dealing with my employees and independent agents as their leader, my goal is to provide the kind of clarity that makes it easy for them to execute tasks with precision. They need the kind of clarity that never leaves them confused, wondering what they should do next.

They need the kind of clarity and certainty that makes them never want to work with anyone else.

This clarity creates an environment based on trust, full disclosure and full transparency.

Achieving Ultimate Clarity

Every small business, regardless of the industry, can benefit from these principles because they are not industry-specific.

If you're in a business where you have to deal with people, manage emotions, lead from the front, and build a true culture (which every small business needs to do), then employing these strategies will enhance your business.

Since I wrote the *First Edition* of this book, I've consulted insurance carriers, insurance agencies, software companies, payroll companies, real estate agencies, medical groups, marketing companies, and a variety of clients from different backgrounds and different industries.

They all needed the same thing: Clarity in regards to what to do next, and how to do it.

You also need this same ultimate clarity.

Without this clarity, you will live the rest of your business life feeling frustrated over 80% of the time, and in my opinion, that's no way to live.

Once you know exactly what to do and exactly how to do it, things become easy to do. Personally speaking, when I don't know how to do something, I get confused.

When I get confused, I get frustrated.

When I get frustrated, I feel overwhelmed.

When I feel overwhelmed, I procrastinate.

Now, you don't have to be a genius or have a Ph.D. in human psychology to know that frustrated, overwhelmed people don't perform very well.

They don't perform well in sports.

They don't perform well in social settings.

And they sure as heck don't perform well in business.

Here's an example of what I mean.

Eleven years ago when my son Estevan was born, our friends and family showered him with gifts.

To give you some perspective on how many gifts I'm talking about, my wife Emilia had four separate baby showers. We got duplicate sets of just about everything. We are very blessed to have so many people in our lives that love us.

That's the good news.

The bad news was that someone had to assemble all of these toys, and unfortunately, that someone was me.

The first box I opened was a baby bouncer. It was a relatively simple apparatus: only about seven parts with a baggy filled with a few nuts and bolts. This was not a complex apparatus, so I figured the assembly would be relatively easy.

Oh, was I wrong.

The first thing I did was open the pamphlet with the assembly instructions in them. They were so confusing that I seriously thought that the manufacturer had made a mistake and put the wrong instructions in with the product.

When I realized the model number on the instructions matched up with the model number on the box, I thought to myself, "Who wrote these crappy instructions?"

I was confused.

I was frustrated.

And I procrastinated.

I just sat there and stared at those stupid instructions for about ten minutes, then crumpled them up, threw them across the room, and yelled out several obscenities. Then I took a nap.

When I woke up from my nap – frustrated and downright angry – I decided to attempt to figure it out on my own by looking at the picture of the fully-assembled baby bouncer on the box.

What should have only taken me fifteen minutes to assemble took me over an hour, and I was not a happy camper.

Now, think about your business. Think about how you train new employees and 1099 agents.

Are they having a frustrating baby bouncer assembly experience?

Remember my definition of clarity?

In business, clarity answers two very important questions:

1. What exactly should I do right now?
2. How exactly should I do it?

Do your agents know exactly what to say to a prospect to book an appointment?

Now, when I say, exactly, I mean exactly.

Do they have a word-for-word verbatim script that has been proven to book appointments, and do you have the statistical data reports to back it up?

Do they know what the target booking percentage has proven to be over time?

Do they know exactly how to read the script? Are they taught about speech inflection—which words to emphasize and where the pregnant pauses should be?

Are they taught the psychology behind every word?

Are they taught how to break the prospect's current emotional state and how to transition them into the appropriate emotional state to increase the booking percentage through specific words and phrases embedded in the script that communicate to the subconscious mind of the prospect?

Once they book the appointment, have you given them a step-by-step process to confirm that appointment?

Is there a step-by-step process to execute that appointment?

Do they know exactly what to say in that first appointment, and is it scripted?

In other words, do they have specific, step-by-step chronology of benefits, inside stories, and testimonials embedded in that first appointment script?

If you don't have these specific, premeditated processes dialed in with every employee at your company, then you don't have a system.

If there is no system, there is going to be a lack of clarity.

And what happens when human beings have a lack of clarity?

They get frustrated.

They get overwhelmed.

They procrastinate.

And if they are new agents, they'll eventually quit.

You may be thinking, "Geez, do I have to show them how to do every little thing, even things that are so obvious?"

The answer, if you want to build a successful insurance agency empire, is yes.

This can be very frustrating for you in the beginning because creating step-by-step, dummy-proof systems is not easy and extremely time consuming.

But the beautiful thing is that once it's done, it's done, and your stress level will get cut in half once a great system is designed and implemented.

Once a great system is running things (and it should run about 80% to 90% of your entire business), you don't have to babysit your business like you are right now.

The system does the babysitting for you, but only if you design it properly with clear directives that give your people ultimate clarity.

Insurance agencies will often hire me as a consultant to design a top-to-bottom agency management system for them, defining every single process and task within their agency.

So let's take a quick reality check.

If you're the boss, sales manager, agency owner or General Agent, are your employees and agents having a frustrating *baby bouncer assembly experience* because they've never been given such detailed, specific directives?

And what about you?

Are you having a frustrating *baby bouncer assembly experience* in your own business life because you don't have a systematized approach to execute your own tasks, as well as an *Agency Protocol Playbook*?

If you're an independent agent, are you having a frustrating *baby bouncer assembly experience* because the parent company you represent has never given you a simple, step-by-step system to follow wherein you have ultimate clarity?

I think we both know the answers to these questions.

Don't feel bad.

Outside of *McDonalds*, *In-And-Out Burger* and *Starbucks* (and a very small handful of other companies), I've never seen a *System-Driven Business* that functions in the way I'm describing.

Your goal should be to get your business dialed in with these systems I'm talking about so that instead of trying to invent the wheel while your wagon is moving (and about to crash), you can spend more time enjoying the ride while your business system chauffeurs you around.

That's why you started your agency in the first place, right?

Yes, you'll make millions of dollars by implementing these systems, but that's not the only reason you want to do this.

The main reason having a *System-Driven Business* is so valuable is it allows you to enjoy your own life, not having every little thing fall on your shoulders every day of the week.

It's too heavy a burden for any person to bear.

Build the system and the system will build the company, instead of you having to lay each brick by hand, one by one.

In this book, I will teach you how I built my initial group health insurance agency from the ground up, how I've built three more agencies since then, and how to avoid all of the stupid mistakes I've made along the way.

CHAPTER 2

MY FIRST YEAR IN IN THE INSURANCE BUSINESS

I think a lot of people look at the companies I've built, and assume that I started out with some sort of special advantage.

If anything, it was just the opposite.

It absolutely makes me cringe when I hear people say, "You have to *have* money to *make* money."

That's nonsense.

When I first started out, I was broke.

Yes, I was driving a *Mercedes*, but don't be impressed.

It was a twelve-year-old *190E* that had over 109,000 miles on it. The dashboard was all cracked up from the sun, and the black carpet in the back window was so faded that it took on a greenish-brown tone.

One day it died on me, so I took it to the repair shop. The repair guy told me that it was going to cost $3,500 to fix it, but the car was worth less than the cost of repairing it. I ended up selling it to a junkyard for $900.

So there I was with no car and no money to buy a new one.

A friend of mine loaned me his extra car, a *Saab* convertible.

Again, don't be impressed. It was thirteen years old.

The week after I started driving it, the clutch went out and I had to cough up $550 on my credit card to get it fixed. A week later, the car broke down in front of my new girlfriend's house in Pasadena around one o'clock in the morning, and I had to use her AAA membership card to tow my car back to Huntington Beach, which was about an hour away.

Great way to impress a new girlfriend.

She was a runway supermodel, and she was used to dating all these big-money Hollywood-type guys. And here I was, with a busted up car and no money.

At that time, I was basically living off of credit cards. But hey, that's what every aspiring entrepreneur does in the beginning when they're trying to get their business going.

It comes with the territory.

Most of my friends lived in Los Angeles, whereas I was living in Orange County. On the weekends, I'd drive up to LA and join them for dinner and drinks.

Of course I was broke, so I'd eat oatmeal or *Top Ramen* at home before I joined them, and I'd just order water at the restaurant because it was free.

At the end of the night, sometimes I'd stay at my friend Tommy's place. He had a studio apartment on the outskirts of Beverly Hills, and he usually stayed at his girlfriend Janine's place on the weekends. He gave me a key to his place, so I'd often crash there.

But sometimes Janine would stay at Tommy's, which meant that I didn't have a place to crash, so I'd drive into Beverly Hills, park on the darkest street I could find, and sleep in my car.

It was cold during the winter time, so I'd sleep in this big, puffy ski jacket, two pairs of socks, and two pairs of sweat pants.

The next morning, I'd sneak into *24-Hour Fitness* with an expired membership ID card to take a shower, brush my teeth, and then head off to my *satellite office*.

My *satellite office* was *The Coffee Bean* (a coffee shop in Los Angeles where the *cool* people hung out) on the corner of Robertson and Beverly Boulevard, right up the street from Tommy's apartment.

There was usually some good eye candy to look at – actresses, models, starlets – as well as wannabe Hollywood writers and wannabe directors. If you've ever seen the TV series *Entourage*, this was the area the show took place in.

Most of my Sundays would be spent on my laptop computer at *The Coffee Bean*, working on new sales scripts, developing marketing ideas, and coming up with new recruiting strategies.

I'd be there from sun-up to sun-down, working, developing and creating.

I didn't have a *real* office yet because I couldn't afford one.

So, my satellite office was *The Coffee Bean* in Beverly Hills, and my main office was the lobby of *The Four Seasons Hotel* in Newport Beach.

It felt rich and luxurious, and of course it was free.

I'd park my car across the street at the *Fashion Island* mall and walk over to the hotel because I couldn't afford the valet parking.

I'd walk into the lobby wearing my suit and tie, carrying an empty briefcase. The people at the front desk probably thought I was some successful businessman staying at the hotel.

Little did they know I was flat broke, using their lobby as my *office*. This is where I did my recruiting interviews, my sales trainings and my team meetings.

It was accessible.

It was luxurious.

And it was free.

Belief In The Impossible

Thank God I was naïve enough to believe in the impossible.

If you've ever heard the expression *act as if*, that was me, acting as if I was some big time insurance tycoon, when in reality, I was flat broke and didn't have any signs of success in my life.

I was trying to reinvent the traditional insurance agency model from scratch. I had all of these crazy ideas about how I thought I could create an entirely different model, and whenever you attempt to do something unconventional that hasn't ever been done before, you go through a lot of trial and error – emphasis on error.

I tried all kinds of different strategies to generate business.

I established referral relationships with financial services firms, life insurance agencies and payroll companies.

On paper, it all looked great.

The problem was that none of these relationships generated very many referrals, and the referrals that it *did* generate didn't turn into clients.

I finally said, "Forget all this affinity partnership crap. Let's just get on the phones and start cold-calling."

I went out and talked a high-rise building manager into leasing us a small office space. It was on the ninth floor of a Class-A office building with a killer view of Newport Beach.

I couldn't afford the office rent at the time, but I borrowed enough money to float me for twelve months. Back then, it was easy to walk into a bank and get a $50,000 unsecured line of credit, so I got a couple of them.

With $100,000 of *Wells Fargo* and *Bank of America's* money in my pocket, I was ready to roll.

At this point, it was do or die.

I installed the desks and the phones myself over the weekend. The desks were cheap $100 desks from *Ikea*, and the phones were cheap $25 phones. I had a screwdriver, some duct tape, and a whole lot of ambition.

My agents came in on Monday and I communicated to them my master plan. It was time to blaze the phones and book appointments in a way that no one in our industry was doing.

I had a great cold-calling script, but I couldn't get my agents to pick up the phone and dial.

Why?

Because most people have an aversion to cold-calling.

It doesn't *feel* professional.

I even had some of my agents tell me, "Darren, I didn't come to work for you to be a telemarketer."

Even though I talked about the bigger picture, they still didn't want to cold call.

Then, things got worse.

One of my agents had a website that he used to market vacation trips to Baja California, and he posted a *Save Money On Health Insurance* advertisement on his website.

Back then, having a website was a big deal. You couldn't just throw up a website for $10 a month like you can today, so not a lot of people had a website – certainly not insurance agents.

Of course, he had to show everyone in my office, and before I knew it, everyone was coming to me wanting a damn website. They thought all they had to do was put up a website and the phones would start ringing off the hook.

With no understanding of SEO or web traffic strategy, they all thought a website was the key to their success.

Then I had one of my agents meet another broker that claimed they were getting rich selling Individual & Family health insurance plans by nailing *Save Money On Your Health Insurance* signs onto telephone poles on busy streets.

Of course, my agent listened to this guy instead of me, so she went out on the weekends and nailed signs onto telephone poles, even though I advised her not to do it.

Eventually, she got one-too-many blood blisters from hammering her own thumb too many times, and she finally gave up on the telephone pole advertising idea.

Here I had this great prospecting script, but no one would use it… until one agent finally listened to me and got some results.

This kid was right out of college with no sales experience.

In fact, on his first day I trained him personally, along with three other brand-new agents.

I reviewed the script with him and the other agents and told them to start calling.

Years later, he confessed to me that it even took him over twenty minutes to pick up the phone and make the first dial.

Why did it take him so long?

Because this kid was a human being just like everybody else, and human beings fear the unknown.

The difference between successful people and unsuccessful people is that successful people take action despite their fear of the unknown.

I first told him that it would take some time to get his commissions built up, but if he stuck with me long enough, he'd develop an incredible career with me. He believed in my vision, and that's exactly what happened.

When I wrote the *First Edition* of this book, he had been with me for over six years and had become my right-hand man at my firm.

From the very beginning, he identified himself as a potential leader, but I had to teach him about leadership and the importance of building a company culture.

Building a company culture is one of the most important things necessary in building a super agency – or any business, for that matter.

Your people have to want to be part of something bigger than themselves, and that type of team mindset is only developed through developing a company culture.

A strong culture defines your company's:

1. Value system.
2. Mission.
3. Brand.

Your company culture dictates how your people think, how they walk, how they talk, how they dress, and how they operate.

A strong company culture has rules, and these rules must be established, articulated, and embraced from the very beginning.

Grinding It Out

At the end of the day, most of our people left the office around 5:00 P.M., but that's when I kicked it into overdrive.

In most high-rise buildings, they turn the air conditioning off towards the end of the day, so at night, my office got extremely hot.

I'd lock the front door, take off my suit and tie (including my pants), and I worked in my underwear until midnight – sometimes until 1:00 A.M.

On the drive home from the office in the middle of the night, I would have conversations with myself, trying to talk myself into believing I was going to be successful.

Sometimes you have to give yourself a pep talk when there's no one else to give you one.

I was working fifteen to sixteen-hour days, seven days a week.

It was now September 2003, and despite my obsessive work schedule for nine months straight, I didn't have much to show for my efforts.

September's gross commissions to my firm totaled a whopping $287, and that was before I paid out commission splits to my agents.

Yes, you read that number correctly.

My entire firm was only generating $287 per month.

My office overhead in that small little office was over $7,000 per month including office rent, our receptionist's salary, and basic business expenses.

I was going deeper and deeper in debt. My credit cards were maxed out, and my lines of credit with *Wells Fargo* and *Bank of America* were almost completely tapped out.

I thought to myself, "My business isn't growing, I'm dead broke, and I don't even know if I'm ever going to be successful at this. Maybe starting this stupid insurance agency was a bad idea."

A lot of people don't believe me when I talk about these beginning stages of my career.

They can't imagine me being depressed about business because they only see my business for what it is today.

They can't imagine me lacking confidence either.

But I started out like every other aspiring entrepreneur filled with the emotional juxtaposition of adrenaline-fueled excitement and paralyzing fear.

Success and confidence take time to build, as does profit. People that have never started a business from scratch with real overhead have no understanding of just how stressful this is.

Even once you start making some decent revenue, you still have to service all the debt you incurred during the initial ramp up period, which can take years just to break even.

Meanwhile, everyone thinks you're successful and that money isn't an issue for you, especially your employees. But any *real* entrepreneur knows that in the beginning stages of any start-up, your expenses are always greater than your revenue, and you can only last for so long before you go belly up and lose everything.

Unless you're a *trust fund baby*, your beginning days of entrepreneurship are filled with struggles, anxiety and doubt (to put it mildly). Every night you go to bed, you're acutely aware that statistically, you have over a 90% chance of failure, and that you are on the brink of bankruptcy and financial ruin.

After my first full year in the insurance business, I almost cracked. I thought about all of the business models I'd tried and failed at. I thought about all the blood, sweat, and tears I had put into trying to build my agency.

And there I was, with less than 300 bucks of revenue coming in the door each month, office overhead I couldn't afford, and six-figures of debt hanging over my head.

My personal income for the entire year of 2003 was $277. Below is a copy of my personal tax return for that year.

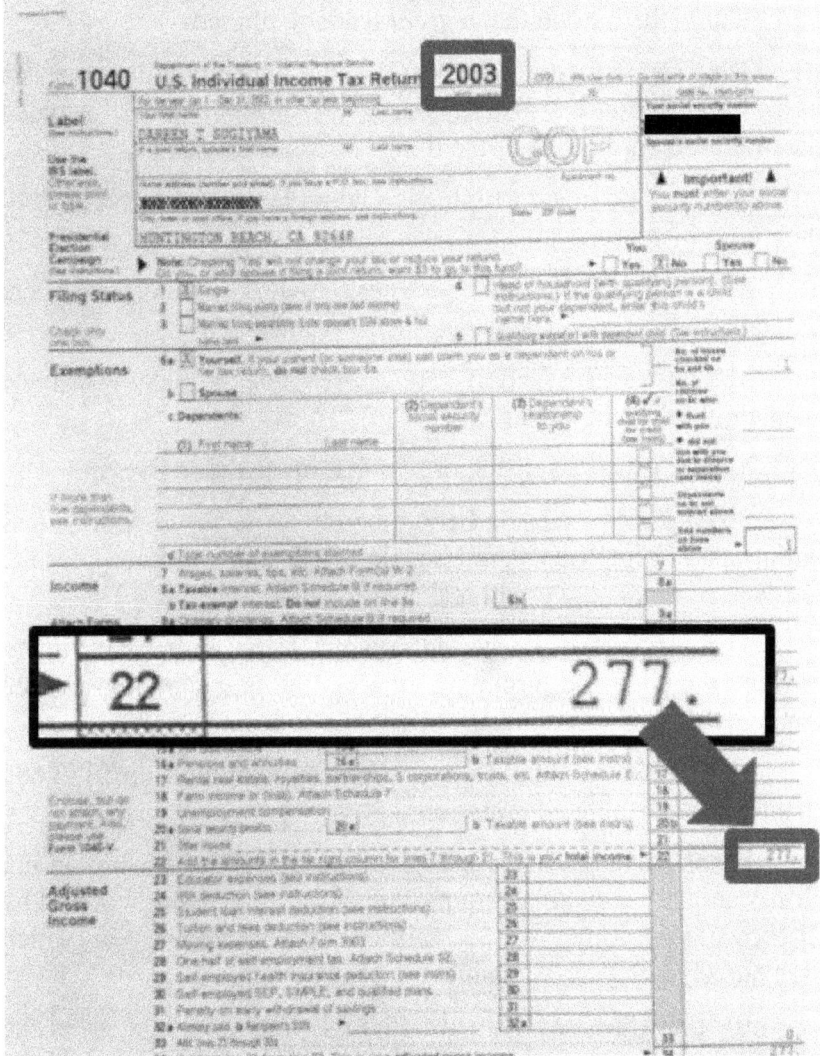

I felt like such a loser.

It's one thing to feel like a loser because you haven't reached the level of success you've always wanted to reach, but it's another thing to shoulder the burden of promising other people that you will lead them to the *Promised Land,* and all the while, you're worried about not being able to pay rent the next month.

But that's the burden that a *true* leader accepts.

That's the burden that a *great* leader embraces.

They say that you can tell a lot about a man based on the size of his dreams, but they also say that you can tell the size of a man's dream based on the size of the things that can steal it.

I've seen so many people give up on their dreams because of their circumstances.

Maybe it was a group of negative friends or family members that talked them out of pursuing their dreams.

Maybe it was a negative spouse that nagged them and made them doubt their potential.

Maybe it was a setback or two that made them give up.

Setback after setback, I continued to forge ahead with no less enthusiasm or intensity than I had on my first day, because despite our lack of revenue, I could feel a shift happening.

That next year, we started crushing it because I had finally cracked the code and turned my *process* into a *system* that I could teach my agents to replicate.

Just twelve months later in 2004, my firm built up $370,685 in annual renewable commissions.

I took quantum leaps the next year in 2005, building up my firm's annual renewable commissions to over $1.3 million, and by 2010, we were doing over $37 million in premium per year, which was our seventh year in business.

By that time, my firm was the #1 producing agency in the entire country with *Health Net, Kaiser Permanente* and *Colonial Life,* all in the same year.

We were the #2 producing agency in California with *Aetna,* #22 with *Blue Cross* in California, and #1 in Orange County with *Blue Shield.*

All of this happened concurrently within a 2-year window, which tells you just how much business we were doing.

We didn't stuff all our business with one carrier.

We spread it around, and even then, we were still at the top of the totem pole with each of these carriers.

In fact, during the 2008 Beijing Olympics, Kaiser Permanente took me as their guest.

To give you an idea of how exclusive this was, they only took me and two other brokers on this trip. We sat in the third row at the closing ceremonies, and to give you an idea of how exclusive these seats were, Vince Vaughn (the movie star from *Wedding Crashers* and *Swingers*) was sitting fifteen rows behind me.

Imagine that. I had better seats at the Olympics than a movie star. That put a big smile on my face.

While in Beijing, the *Kaiser Permanente* Executive Team and I also met with the *Ministry Of Health* – the governing body of China's entire healthcare system – to discuss the future of healthcare in both of our countries.

I was only 36-years old at the time.

It was a true honor to participate in such a prestigious meeting.

There were three main components that made this *System-Driven Business* scalable.

Key Component #1: Recruiting.

The first key component was our ability to recruit agents.

In our business, it takes several months to ramp up, and at the beginning of an insurance agent's career, it's a financial struggle.

You have to find people that believe in the bigger picture dream and are willing to sacrifice in the short-term.

I knew that we needed to find people that wanted to be financially successful, but more importantly, we needed people that wanted to be part of something special – something bigger than themselves.

I focused on developing a culture of people that truly wanted to help our clients, and we made no apologies for pointing out all of the wrongdoings other brokers were committing against their clients, which was not a difficult thing to do.

So many brokers kept their clients in the dark regarding creative ways to reduce the cost of their insurance premiums.

There were only two reasons why this was happening.

One, the broker didn't have the knowledge of how to strategically formulate a better employee benefits package using new tax codes and new consumer-driven health plans, thus resulting in the client overpaying.

Or two, the broker was lazy and wanted to maximize their commissions at the expense of their client.

These untalented, lazy brokers were making hundreds of thousands of dollars by keeping their clients in the dark.

I quickly realized that if that's what the majority of brokers were doing, then all we had to do was expose these wrongdoings and show clients their true options.

In *Chapter 3: Becoming A Master Recruiter* I will go into intimate detail regarding how to recruit the right agents.

Key Component #2: The Prospecting Script.

The second key component was the refinement of our prospecting script. Our initial success came from a 100% cold-calling model.

I refined our script to the point where I knew exactly how many appointments my script would book per week based on quantifiable statistics.

Virtually everyone I put on the phones with this magical script booked the same amount of appointments.

Once I perfected this process, I was halfway there.

My agents booked so many appointments that they went from feeling like desperate sales people, to having prospects begging them for help. I was personally running twenty to twenty-five sales appointments per week, and things were finally coming together.

Key Component #3: The Culture.

The third key component was developing an agency culture.

I had six agents that said they wanted to be part of my culture. Of the six, two of them turned out to be absolute nightmares, and one of them, though a really nice guy, just didn't put in the effort required to be successful.

However, the other three really took off like rocket ships, and those three producers were the catalyst of what would eventually become a $37 million agency.

This was the beginning of establishing a true culture.

In order to build a company culture, one person needs to lead the charge in your organization, and that person is usually going to be you.

If you can find one person to buy into your vision, your values, your belief system, and your standard method of operation, then you've got a team captain. If you and that team captain can just get one more agent to buy into these beliefs, you have a culture.

All you need is three strong members subscribing to your culture – just three. At that point, every new person you bring into your organization will assimilate into your culture.

That's how you build your initial momentum.

So the one-two-three punch was:
1. Recruit good people that wanted to work hard.
2. Train them to read the script.
3. Build our culture.

I suffered a miserable start in 2003, my first year of business. In that year, my agency generated a whopping $592.73, and that's before I paid the commission splits out to my producers.

Yes, you read that number correctly.

My agency made less than $600 in total gross commissions for the entire year. You saw my personal tax return a few pages ago with the $277 of annual income.

A lot of people ask me why I share these numbers so openly with the public.

The reason is that so many people feel like failures in their first couple of years in the insurance business, and seeing how little income I made in the beginning of my career often times gives them the confidence and hope they need to continue.

Everyone progresses at a different speed, and the one that gets off to the *fastest start* is not always the one that builds the *biggest empire*.

So, people ask me all the time, "How did you do it? How did you build such a successful business in such a short amount of time?"

In this book, I'm going to share with you some of my most valuable secrets of how I did it.

But remember, this is the *Second Edition* version of this book that I published a decade ago, so not only will I explain my initial strategies I used from the very beginning, I'll also share with you my perspectives on those initial strategies from a retrospective viewpoint.

Some of the contents from the *First Edition* are still relevant, of which I still employ to this day ten years later.

Some of the contents I cut out due to updating, refreshing and recalibrating my business model over the last ten years.

And some of the new content in this *Second Edition* are game changing and significantly more sophisticated than what my 10-years younger self wrote about in 2010.

One area that has changed significantly is the way I go about recruiting and onboarding new agents, which I will address in this next chapter.

CHAPTER 3
BECOMING A MASTER RECRUITER

A *Master Recruiter* doesn't contract as many agents as they possibly can.

A *Master Recruiter* identifies the *right* candidates that are the *right* fit for their organization.

There are some interviewees you should pass on.

You're looking for driven people that understand that there is far greater upside potential in a performance-based, straight-commission position, compared to a job with a fixed base salary.

If you want to be a *Master Recruiter*, you need to be blunt regarding how tough the beginning stages of this career are.

You'll turn off over 80% of the interview candidates, but that's exactly what you want to do. Those people would have never survived on straight-commission because they just aren't cut out for it. They can't take rejection and they aren't willing to suffer the discomfort of going these tough and lean beginning stages of a career with no base salary.

You want your entire message to be focused on providing clarity for the 20% that *think* they want the big time.

Of this 20%, half of them will decide that as enticing as the opportunity sounds, they can't take the uncertainty of a straight-commission position and they'll remove themselves from the interview process.

This leaves you with the remaining 10% that *say* they are adamant about wanting to be an entrepreneur.

Still, just because someone *says* they want to be an entrepreneur doesn't mean they're willing to do what it takes to endure the *lean* early years that a straight-commission position comes with. They'll tell you they understand that it doesn't happen overnight and they'll tell you all the right things you want to hear.

45

But don't get excited. Of this remaining 10%, half of them are just big talkers.

These people will tell you how this is the perfect career for them and how amazing you are. You will fall victim to flattery and you'll get all excited about your seemingly ambitious new recruit. But when they disappear and stop returning your emails, you'll be emotionally crushed.

Perhaps you have already experienced this.

Don't fall for the big talkers. Talk is cheap.

Look for action.

The action will come from the remaining 5%.

This is the 5% you want to target.

If you just shoot straight with this 5% and provide them clarity as to what they'll be doing and how they'll be doing it, the right candidates will gladly join your team.

The other 95% of the people that you interview just aren't cut out for this. You'd be wasting your time if you tried to convince them to join your team.

Recruiting isn't about contracting the *most* interviewees. It's about contracting the *right* interviewees.

The *Master Recruiter* interviews as many candidates as possible in search of the right players that fall into that 5% niche and only contracts them.

Let's do the numbers.

Out of every twenty interviewees, 80% of them won't be interested after the first interview because they know they wouldn't do what it takes to be successful in our industry. They'll voluntarily remove themselves from the interview process. That means only four of them will come back for a second interview.

Of the four, two of them will realize that even though they were excited about the opportunity initially, they just can't go without a base salary.

Of the two that are left standing, one of them will tell you how perfect they are for this type of opportunity and how they'll do whatever it takes to be successful.

Whenever someone tells you they'll do whatever it takes to be successful, run for the hills. Everyone that has ever told me this was a *dreamer*.

Don't go for the *dreamers*.

Go for the *doers*.

I've found that the more they talk about what they're going to do, the less they end up doing. The more they tell you how much they *need* this opportunity, the less chance they have what it takes.

I know a lot of agency owners and sales team leaders tell their people to *dream big*, and they love hearing about their agents' dreams of grandeur.

I certainly used to preach this myself.

But forget all of that nonsense.

You want the people that make more *moves* and less *announcements*.

Job Postings

Your job posting must be unique.

It must be written in a way that jumps off the page, differentiating you from all of the other job postings.

Most job postings are boring all sound the same. They talk about how long the company has been in business, their *Better Business Bureau* rating, and a bunch of non-needle moving fluff. None of these things make the job searcher curious to find out more.

If you're looking for straight-commissioned sales people, your job posting should include in its description very specific things about your corporate culture and your office environment.

For example, "If you don't want to live in a cubicle the rest of your life, begging for a raise you'll never get, this may be the opportunity for you."

These things don't sound *professional*, but they do sound compelling, which is your entire goal.

You should also have a link to your website on the job posting.

Now, that being said, your recruiting website must be compelling and out-of-the-ordinary. By the way, your recruiting website should be different than your main company website.

Your recruiting website (which may be a hidden landing page within your main company website) should have video testimonials given by your employees, your agents, and by carrier executives.

You need to have third-party validation for credibility purposes, because unless you're marketing yourself under the banner of a well-known company, no one's ever heard of your independent boutique agency.

New York Life or *Northwestern Mutual*, yes.

Joe Blow Insurance Agency, no.

Video testimonials are key because they give you that much needed third-party validation, and statistically speaking, people will watch a video before they will read long text copy.

Back when I wrote the *First Edition* of this book, I talked extensively about the importance of videos, not only for recruiting purposes, but also in the sales process, which I will elaborate on later in this book.

Scheduling Interviews

There are three major rules I have when it comes to my interview process.

Rule #1: Never talk to a job candidate prior to the interview.

This is the worst thing you can do.

The candidate is going to grill you with a million questions. And what is the recruiter going to end up doing?

They're going to answer every question as they get grilled.

They ask things like, "What's the base salary?" or, "How many hours a week do I have to work?" or, "Do you offer benefits and health insurance?"

The problem with these questions is that they can't be answered in totality on a five-minute phone call.

If they call my office prior to the interview, my assistant is instructed to say, "You'll actually be interviewing with Mr. Sugiyama himself, and he will address all of your questions at that time."

So here's my step-by-step pre-interview process.

My assistant receives e-mails from candidates that are responding to the online job posting. If the candidate calls my office wanting information, they are directed to e-mail my assistant. My assistant has half-a-dozen pre-authored email template responses that she copies-and-pastes because there are only half-a-dozen categorical questions a candidate will have.

I only do interviews once a week in a group, so the date and time is already pre-set. If the candidate requests a different date or time, my assistant copies-and-pastes this reply:

> "This is the only time Mr. Sugiyama has available this week, and he is making decisions at the end of this week. If you can rearrange your schedule to accommodate, please confirm your attendance. If you cannot, we wish you the best of luck in your future endeavors."

I do not accommodate alternative interview scheduling requests. If they cannot accommodate my schedule, I pass.

Why am I so adamant about this?

Because I've allowed candidates to control the process in the past, back when I was an *Amateur Recruiter*, and it never panned out well. Not once. You need to establish your status as the *pursued*, not the *pursuer*.

Rule #2: Never do a first interview one-on-one.

I only do group interviews for first interviews.

The reason is that I have no idea whether I'm going to like the interviewee prior to the interview. A résumé can only tell you so much about the candidate.

I used to interview people one-on-one for the first interview, but the problem was that I would block out a full hour for each interviewee. If I didn't like the interviewee, I lost that hour of productive time because I had to wait for the next interviewee to come in an hour later.

Plus, the no-show rate of interviewees is typically around 70%. Only 30% of the scheduled interviewees even show up.

In a group interview, I never waste time on an unqualified interviewee because I'm meeting with the entire group at one time.

The other problem I experienced was that many of these one-on-one interviewees came in with an attitude, as if *they* were interviewing *me*.

I actually felt as though I had to *sell* them on the opportunity.

Now, if you've ever been to any of my trainings, workshops, or seminars, you know that one of my rules is that I refuse to chase anyone, and I hate trying to convince anyone to do anything.

If you're in the *convincing game*, then you're in a position of weakness.

When my assistant schedules a group interview, she confirms 20 to 25 interviewees for this time slot.

70% of them will no-show. No problem. That means 4 to 8 will show up.

Since the *First Edition* of this book, the no-show rate has increased substantially. Ten years ago, the numbers were inversed with a 30% no-show rate, and 70% would show. At the time of me writing this *Second Edition* (2020), at least 70% of interview candidates that confirm their interview attendance will not show up.

So if you want 4-8 butts in seats, you need to get attendance confirmations from approximately 20 candidates.

In the group interview, I talk about the industry, our systematized approach, our mentorship and development program, and the three qualities I look for in interviewees.

The three qualities I'm looking for are:

1. Raw intelligence
2. Work ethic
3. Coachability

These are three qualities that I cannot teach.

They are characteristics that I believe are part of the person's DNA. I can't teach someone to be smart. If they lack intellectual capacity, there's really nothing I can do about it.

If they're lazy, they're lazy. Laziness is a character flaw that is part of who that person is. I'll tell candidates right off the bat that if they're not ready to be a semi-workaholic for the next two years, this type of career is not for them.

I always say a straight-commission insurance agent either has the easiest highest-paying gig, or the hardest lowest-paying gig. There's no in-between.

I don't tell them they *have* to start and end their day at a certain time (which I elaborate on in *Chapter 9* regarding 1099 compliance), but I will tell them that it's only worth my time to invest in people that want to obsess about their career the way I obsess about my career. I'm looking for equally-yolked running mates, not average people that want mediocre results.

This brings me to the third quality I'm looking for.

Coachability.

A new agent must be an excellent student of our system.

If the agent has an over-inflated opinion of themselves and they're not willing to run my system to the tee, it will be a waste of my time. They will fail, and neither of us will make a dime.

It always cracks me up when a rookie tells me that they want to do it *their way*.

I just tell them, "If you want to use my proven method, I'll teach you how to run my system. If not, no problem. I wish you the best of luck in your career. It just won't be here with me."

I know my system works, and I know that most agents left to their own devices will most likely fail, so I don't have the time or the patience to work with an uncoachable agent.

I try to scrub these people out in the interview process.

Rule #3: Attempt to scare away 80% of the candidates in the first interview.

Tell the group that statistically, you only take on 5% of the candidates that come in for the interview, and that the interview process is to figure out whether or not they are part of that 5%.

Tell them that only 20% of the candidates even get invited back for a second one-on-one interview.

Then tell them how hard the beginning stages of this career are, and how most people aren't cut out for it, but the ones that are get rich.

The goal is to scrub out 80% of the group as soon as possible.

I will now explain my step-by-step interview process.

The First Impression

The first impression you make on an interview candidate is incredibly important. I always have interviewees wait a minimum of five minutes in the foyer.

Why?

Because I want them to soak in the environment. I want them to look at our office and our people. I want them to listen the music I have playing in the office, tuned at 432 hz. I want them to read the testimonial letters I have in our portfolio in the foyer.

I want them to get a feel of our culture, reinforcing the image they experienced on our website through our videos.

The candidates should be waiting in the foyer, anticipating the unknown. This lends to the mystique of our operation. They are then escorted into the conference room for the group interview.

Ideally, there should be four to eight interviewees in a group interview. Any more than eight interviewees starts to feel like a cattle call. Even if many of the confirmed interviewees flake out and no-show, it's not a problem.

I've done interviews with just two candidates in a group interview, and it's still very effective.

Prior to me stepping into the conference room to begin the group interview, the interviewees watch an eight-minute video about our firm. It's loaded with testimonials of insurance carrier executives talking about my agency as well as some of my agents talking about what it's like to work with me and the success they've achieved with me.

By the time I step into the room, the credibility factor is a nonissue. In fact, the video actually creates a celebrity effect for me, which positions me differently on a first-meet.

The video sets the stage for the group interview.

In addition to articulating our agency brand, the video also communicates my personal brand. These people want to know that they're following someone that's worth following.

The interview video must articulate both brands.

Introductions

I start by telling each candidate to pass their résumés forward. The confirmation email my assistant sent them prior to the interview instructed them to bring a printed copy of their résumé to the interview.

I then tell them to introduce themselves with their name, where they're from, and why they specifically wanted to interview with us.

I have been known to dismiss interview attendees immediately after their introduction if they did not bring their résumé, or if my front desk people tell me an interviewee wasn't paying attention to the video.

If they don't give me a specific reason of why they wanted to interview with me, and they don't know anything about our firm, despite the confirmation email specifically instructing them to watch one of the testimonial videos on our website, I will dismiss them on the spot as well.

It may sound harsh, but this gets the lesser caliber interviewees out of the room so they don't poison the good ones. It also sends a message to the other interviewees that this is not a cattle call.

This is an interview, and I am looking for a specific type of candidate.

Most cattle call group interviews send the wrong message to top producers. If you have a real *hitter* in the interview, they will be turned off by the *we'll take anyone with a heartbeat* recruiting process.

I'm also looking to see how the interviewees present themselves when speaking in front of their peers (the other interviewees).

For the remainder of the group interview, I talk about the opportunity. I don't ask them any more questions about themselves. I save that for the second interview, which is done in a one-on-one environment.

The group interview must have the same exact format every single time. Now, if you've read any of my other books or attended my seminars, you know I'm a script-guy, so of course, my group interview is script-based.

Here are the topics I discuss at a group interview.

Our Target Market

Our target market has been small-to-medium sized businesses – 10 to 200 employees – and non-industry specific. Our sweet spot has been 10-30 employees, and we only deal with business owners

– no *H.R. Directors* or *Office Managers*. We only meet with the true decision maker – the business owner.

In the group interview, I start off discussing issues that most business owners are faced with, whether they be current economic conditions, personnel issues, or past challenges that are indicative of future challenges to come. I position our unique offerings as tailor-made solutions for these challenges.

I talk about the fact that now more than ever, business owners are open to talking to us about creative ways to save money on their insurance (without sacrificing richness in benefits), as well as protecting their investment portfolio from market crashes.

Both of these past, present and future challenges are opportunities for our prospective clients to form new relationships with my firm due to our unique strategies.

I highlight the fact that the timing has never been better for them to enter this career with us because of these unique solutions we can offer our clients.

It is incredibly important for you to highlight the limited window of opportunity that currently exists to *get in*.

The Type of Work We Do

I then run through two or three case studies of real clients. I show the interviewees how we helped these clients and what the final outcomes were.

Interviewees need to see what type of work they'd be doing. They need to see that we have unique, cutting-edge, proprietary strategies that give us the edge in the marketplace.

This is where your *USP (Unique Selling Proposition)* comes in. Clients need to know why they should do business with you – only you – and nobody else. Likewise, your interviewees also need to know why they should work with you – only you – and nobody else.

In my organization, the number one reason people come to work for us is our mentorship program.

We highlight the fact that they're going to have the opportunity to learn directly from the top agents at our firm – top agents that started out just like them, at ground zero, and worked their way to the top doing exactly what they're going to teach them to do.

This mentorship-based model teaches the new agent every element of the game, hands-on. It also helps to ensure the new agent's success because they have one of my heavy hitters closing business for them in the beginning on a case-split.

They not only witness success, but they also experience it first-hand.

Scrubbing Out Bad Candidates

I know recruiters that will try to talk interviewees into the opportunity by making it sound easier than it actually is. This is a major mistake.

When they find out it's not an easy career path, they'll quit after you've invested all your time and emotion into them. It's a terrible return on investment.

You've probably been making this mistake for years.

If your time was a stock, it would be plummeting right now.

I speak from personal experience on this one.

Now that I've stopped making this mistake, I don't find myself wasting time trying to mentor and train someone that was really never a good fit for my organization in the first place.

All I want to do is clarify what they gain by working with me, and what they lose by not working with me.

My goal by being super blunt is to scare away 80% of the room. At this point in the group interview – which is about twenty minutes in (8 minutes for the video and 12 minutes of explaining what we do) – I will tell them that I am going to step out of the room for two minutes to get some coffee, and that if anyone feels this is not the right opportunity for them, that they can excuse themselves from the interview, and I wish them luck.

When I step back into the room, though my goal was to scare away 80% of them, typically about 50%-60% still remain.

This is when I allow them to ask me questions.

Q&A Session

I wrap up the group interview by allowing six questions to be asked, and I'm very direct and blunt in this session.

I will then bring in one of my top producers to do an additional five-minute *Q&A Session* with the interviewees. Interviewees will always trust what one of your top agents says over what you say.

I will then dismiss myself from the interview.

The Next Step

Once my top producer wraps up the final 5-minute *Q&A Session*, the candidates are instructed to stop at the front desk on their way out to book their second interview if they want to come back.

My assistant stacks the one-on-one interviews two days later, fifteen minutes apart.

Lastly, you want to make sure you wrap up the interview before the interviewees want to leave. You have to leave them wanting more.

You must make sure the *Q&A Session* with your top producer does not last more than five minutes. Often times, your top producers will like the experience of being showcased as the star a little too much, and they'll want to spend more time answering questions because it makes them feel important.

Make sure your assistant yanks them out of there in five minutes because you must leave the interviewees wanting more.

Here's another important post-interview tip.

Never thank an interviewee for coming to an interview, and make sure your top producer doing the final *Q&A* doesn't thank them either.

The interviewee should be thanking you for the opportunity, not the other way around.

They should be trying to convince *you* to take them on.

In this book, I'll be talking a lot about changing the dynamic of interaction between you and your interviewees as well as changing the dynamic of the relationship between you and your clients.

What I've Learned Over The Last 10 Years About Recruiting

Again, the reason I wrote this *Second Edition* of the original version of this book was that several things have changed over the last decade.

The job market has changed.

Pop culture has changed.

The quality of interview candidates has changed.

But most importantly, *I've* changed.

In these last ten years, I've launched several additional businesses that were heavily recruiting-based.

In 2011, I launched another firm – *Pacific Bay Insurance Group* – which was intended to be a sister company to my employee benefits agency, *Apex Outsourcing*.

My wife Emilia, who has been in the insurance game ten years longer than I have, ran the day-to-day operations. *Pacific Bay* specialized in *voluntary benefits*, and sold supplemental insurance products to employees of companies that covered the things that their major medical insurance didn't cover.

We exclusively sold *Colonial Life* products.

In our first year, we won the *Agency Of The Year Award* in Orange County from *Colonial Life*.

Pacific Bay used the same *System-Driven Business* model I originally used with *Apex*. I recruited young recent college graduates, and built our agency up to twenty-two agents in less than a year.

In our second year, *Pacific Bay* was responsible for 58% of the new accounts opened for *Colonial Life* in Orange County and San Bernardino County combined.

In that same year of 2012, I started yet another firm called *DaVinci Financial & Insurance Associates*. I came up with the absurd of idea to sell life insurance to business owners entirely over the phone, cold-calling into 17 different states. We called these business owners at their place of business, during business hours, and even built our own auto-dialer system in-house. I built that agency up to 45 agents in our Irvine office, plus additional offices in Seattle, Dallas, Hartford, Jersey City, Manhattan and Las Vegas.

I was interviewing over 100 agents per week. I held three group interviews per week – Tuesday, Wednesday and Thursday at 10:00 A.M. – with an average of 30 to 40 interviewees per session.

I had completely abandoned my original game plan of being selective in the interviewing and onboarding process, which was a huge mistake.

Remember I said that you're going to learn the greatest lessons from my mistakes instead of my successes?

Well, this is one of them, so pay close attention to what I'm about to share with you regarding what I've learned over the last ten years when it comes to recruiting.

We were onboarding 4-6 new agents per week.

I had fallen victim to the desire to grow too fast.

I went extreme with my brand – too extreme.

My *aspirational brand* had become something reminiscent of *The Boiler Room* or *The Wolf Of Wall Street*, and some of the messaging I was putting out there was far too focused on monetary success.

Everything was centered around this *Look How Successful I Am And You Can Be This Successful Too* brand.

The excuse I convinced myself into believing was that it was all in the spirit of promoting my aspirational brand, and that it would motivate our agents to work harder to be the best.

As you can probably tell by my explanation of this era, I am mildly embarrassed and ashamed of how I promoted this gluttonous, ego-centric image during this time.

We have all done and said some things in our younger years we lived to regret, and I am certainly guilty of doing this during this stage of my business.

In my defense, I had struggled for so long, that once I *made it*, I secretly wanted to rub it in everyone's face as validation for my hard work and sacrifice.

But that's what insecure people do.

As much confidence and bravado as I was putting out there back then, the reality was that my ego felt it was payback time against all my doubters-turned-haters. This mindset is a major indicator of a person's insecurity – and in this case, my insecurity.

I'm certainly not proud of it.

Everyone that truly knows me knows that money, power and materialism are not things I value whatsoever. But there I was, promoting an image that I thought I *had* to promote in order to recruit.

Short-term it worked incredibly well, which is how I tricked myself into believing that it was a good move. But long-term, it wasn't the model I wanted to be associated with. It attracted a bunch of agents that cared more about what car they were driving than character, integrity and honor.

I don't care who you are or how much you think you are immune to this type of egoism. When you are submerged in this type of culture for too long, you start to become someone that cares far too much about impressing other people with your conspicuous consumption. You can easily lose your *true north*.

You become obsessed with having to buy the next car, the next watch, the next fashion item with logos blasted all over it so that everyone can see that you can afford things that they cannot.

I remember a friend of one of my agents said, "If Darren is so successful, how come he only has the *Porsche Panamera 4S*... why didn't he get the *Turbo?*"

So I went out and got the *Ferrari 458*.

"That'll show him!" I secretly said to myself.

A few months later, I found myself at the *Lamborghini* dealership looking at the *Aventador*, because I started feeling like my *Ferrari* wasn't good enough anymore.

Do you see how this becomes a vicious cycle?

All of this nonsense is rooted in insecurity. It is the need to seek external validation from other people, because deep down, we are not fully satisfied with who we are inside.

A truly confident person doesn't need to show off.

To clarify, there's nothing wrong with being a *car guy* or a *watch guy* or a *jewelry/shoe/handbag gal*. If you're an avid collector, or if you just like these things, please don't misinterpret what I'm saying here.

There is nothing wrong with liking nice things. I still like nice things too. It's not like I've become an extreme minimalist or anything. I'm not exactly walking around with a *$10 Casio* watch, driving an economy car either.

I am just speaking from personal experience on this one. Despite being the leader in my organization, I found myself following what I thought other people wanted. Again, it's mildly embarrassing to admit, but I'm just being transparent with you.

Additionally, if the leader is overly focused on promoting this type of brand, their followers will become overly consumed with this desire as well.

This carrot-dangling aspirational strategy works initially because people get excited about the prospect of living the lifestyle of a rockstar, but when the majority of them do not reach this level of success – at no fault of your own as a leader – many of these people will grow to resent you. But that's not even the real problem.

The real problem is that when a person is jealous and covets your success – especially if they are irrational and won't do the work required to become successful – they begin shortcutting the system and rationalizing dishonorable behavior because their desire for the *bling* has been deeply embedded in their subconscious by – you're going to hate this part – your aspirational brand.

This is why I say you must be selective in who you invite to join your team.

If you successfully recruit the masses, you are going to end up with a large population of irrational people that don't do the work required for them to be successful enough to buy all of your diamond-encrusted toys.

The flashy, aspirational brand will work for a season, but when you put out *shit*, you attract the *flies*.

The flies will then lay eggs, and then the maggots hatch.

That's when the real problems start.

I even had one of these shortcut-minded agents tell me, "There are givers and there are takers. We've been *giving* for too long. We need to start *taking*."

I knew at that moment, I could not continue with him.

Back then, my aspirational brand had developed a habit of bringing home these wounded, stray dogs, only to find out they had rabies.

It was all in the spirit of promoting *the dream*, and I really did believe I could make these people successful. I would later find out that you can't turn a pigeon into an eagle.

You need to find baby eagles, not attempt to perform bird species reassignment surgery.

Every time I have attempted to turn a pigeon into an eagle, I have been betrayed, blamed and robbed.

All of that time invested was wasted.

Eventually, they all left anyway, stealing clients that I was largely responsible for them getting in the first place.

Something I Neglected To Articulate In The First Edition

As I pondered one of the criticisms of one of my haters, he actually had a good point – one that I have always agreed with, but apparently something got lost in translation in the *First Edition* version – and I can see how he could have misunderstood something about my recruiting process.

First of all, I would like clarify that I don't care for the terms *recruiting* and *recruiter*.

I use them in this book as well as in the *First Edition* simply because they are industry-standard terms.

But the reason I don't like them is that they are terms usually synonymous with convincing someone to do something for the benefit of the *recruiter*, not for the benefit of the individual being *recruited*.

It's similar to the way I feel about the terms *closing* and *closer*. They just sound like terms associated with manipulation and trickery.

I don't *recruit* agents to break their backs for me so I can make money off of their blood, sweat and tears.

I offer a mentorship opportunity for them to learn from me, where they can observe me successfully executing what I am teaching them to do.

It's hard to imagine that someone could find fault in that model, but they do. This illogical criticism will never go away.

There is a certain minimum level of rational thought a person must have to understand the true value proposition in this type of relationship.

Unfortunately, it is nearly impossible to flush that out in the interview process. You will have some interviewees convince you that they are rational people, only to prove to you otherwise at a later date.

When this happens (and it will happen to you), you have to brush it off and not let it affect you emotionally. I think it's important for every leader to continually do *some* personal production as an agent.

If you've built an agency, I know you may feel like you're *above* this, but if your people start feeling like you're making money *off* them, they will despise you for it.

You must create an environment where you're delivering value to them, where they feel like you're making money *with* them, not *off* of them.

This is easier said than done, and in many cases, you will find yourself attempting to have a rational conversation with an irrational person, which is a waste of time and a losing battle.

Perhaps you were hoping I could give you the magic bullet for this issue, but this irrationality is a different kind of pandemic that there is no vaccine for.

Unfortunately, you're going to have to *suck it up* – and in some cases *lawyer up* – and deal with the small minds of delusional people.

Just remember what Aristotle and Theodore Roosevelt said.

It may not solve the problem, but it will help you deal with the frustration and heartache.

I personally chose to develop a very different business model, but if you decide to forge on with your current model – which may be the right move for you – you must accept that the liability of this type of betrayal and potential mass exodus is always going to be a threat to your business.

That doesn't make it a bad business model, however.

I live in Southern California, which means I pay an insane amount of taxes compared to other states, business laws drastically favor employees over employers, the cost of real estate is among the highest in the country, and it is one of the most superficial societies in the world.

But I still choose to live here in spite of all of this.

Similarly, the right decision for you may be to continue with your current model and not change your course.

Every business is different, and every person's preference is different as well. What's *right* for me may be very different than what's *right* for you.

I have close friends that have different political views, religious views, lifestyles, sexual preferences, cultural norms, beliefs about how to discipline their kids – you name it.

I judge none of them.

I only know what's *right* for me.

In order to develop the *right* business model, you have to do some serious soul searching and decide what's right for you.

Three of the most important questions you can ask yourself – and you have to be completely honest and transparent with yourself about this – are what helped clarify things for me.

1. Who do you really want to be?
2. Why do you want to be that?
3. Assuming you become that, will you be happy, or are you doing it:
    a. For ego gratification?
    b. To make other people happy?
    c. To impress other people?
    d. Because that's what everyone else is doing?

As I took time to deeply think through these questions, my discoveries led me down the road to ultimate clarity – a level of clarity that I thought I had before, but did not ever truly have.

I will share with you many of these life-changing epiphanies throughout this book.

CHAPTER 4

PEOPLE-DRIVEN V. SYSTEM-DRIVEN

I've done quite a bit of high-level business development consulting over the years for an array of different types of companies – some boutique agencies, and some billion-dollar corporations.

Not one of them was *System-Driven*.

They were all *People-Driven*.

The fate of these companies was completely in the hands of their current employees based on the employees' knowledge, skill, relationships, intelligence, and human abilities.

Having talented employees is great. Don't get me wrong.

But if the talent leaves, the value of the company plummets, and replacing talent is not easy.

In an insurance agency, a *People-Driven* business model with no system is a ticking time bomb.

If the people leave, the agency becomes worth nothing.

The only way for an insurance agency to have any *enterprise value* is to have a *system* that is more valuable than the *people*.

Let's talk about your recruiting process and the demographics of your new agent candidates.

Most agencies try to recruit agents with experience and a book of business to bring over because they perceive that training newly-licensed agents is too much work.

If you recruit based on talent and experience, you've got to ask yourself, "If this agent is already such a great producer, why do they want to come and work for me?"

If they're an independent broker and they're making over a quarter of a million dollars a year, they wouldn't be interviewing with you. So if they're not working for another agency, then they're lying to you about their production and their level of past successes.

If they've been working for another agency and they're bragging about their book of business they can bring over, they're looking to leave their old firm and steal clients from the agency that actually owns the book of business.

I can't tell you how many interviewees have told me they've got this big book of business that they want to bring over to my firm.

Right off the bat, they're telling me that they're going to attempt to screw their soon-to-be ex-employer.

If they're the kind of person that is willing to screw their current employer, then it's only a matter of time before they decide to screw you too.

Don't be a sucker.

Don't let your greed overtake your integrity and better judgment. This is a *wolf in sheep's clothing*, and you'll regret bringing this *Trojan Horse* into your agency.

They'll come in with a bunch of sob stories and a lot of baggage, and they'll expect you to be their bell hop.

Listen, if you want to be a professional baggage boy, then go get a part-time job working the curb at the *Ritz Carlton*. At least there you'll make tips.

Now, am I saying that you should never take on people that already have an insurance background?

No, I'm not saying that at all.

If you find an agent that is the right fit for your organization and they're coachable and hungry, fantastic.

Just make sure that they want to run your system, not just *hang their license* with you.

My *System-Driven Business* is responsible for ensuring a new agent's productivity and success, not their talent or their contacts.

If they happen to also be talented and also have contacts, that's great.

There are certainly some talented agents out there that realize they don't have a system – usually a lead generation system – and if they're coming to you in a humble and transparent way looking for a system to run, they could be a great fit for your agency.

Again, you must develop enterprise value, and the only way to develop enterprise value is to have one or more of the following:

1. A lead generation system.
2. A unique delivery system.
3. A proprietary product.
4. A unique company culture and brand that cannot easily be replicated.
5. A *Thought Leader* that agents want to be connected to.

People-Driven businesses tend to hold the agency owner hostage. If your people start feeling like they don't need you or the agency infrastructure anymore, they'll eventually leave you and attempt to rob you blind.

All of your hard work in developing and training them will have been in vain, not to mention both the hard and soft dollars you invested in them.

Content

I'm constantly developing new content for my agents.

What do I mean by content?

New sales scripts.

New sales and marketing videos.

New things that make their job easier and ultimately make them more successful.

You see, my people know that I'm constantly evolving my agency to stay several steps ahead of the competition. This evolution of our operation and systems plays a huge role in our success as an agency, and my people know it.

The entire system – what I call *The System-Driven Business* – is a top-to-bottom clearly delineated process that governs every task that every person in my agency executes, so everyone knows what to do and how to do it.

My agents know exactly what to say on the phone to book a sales appointment. They know exactly what to say when they're on that sales appointment. They know exactly what to do in every scenario imaginable. They know the style and medium in which that message is to be communicated, and they understand the philosophy behind why this method works.

They know exactly what to do and how to do it.

Now, think about your own business. When you take on a brand-new agent, on their first day, do you have a specific step-by-step process to get that agent started?

Think about your veteran agents.

Are they trained in a system that produces virtually the exact same result for every agent that executes that process?

Do they know exactly what to do?

Do they know exactly how to do it?

On a sales call, do they know exactly what to say?

Do they know exactly how to say it?

If the answer to any of these questions is *no*, then you don't have a *System-Driven Business*. You've got a *People-Driven Business*, which by definition, means that your people are being left to their own devices.

And what usually happens when you leave people to their own devices?

They fail miserably.

Now you're miserable.

If you have agents, what percentage of the time do you find yourself frustrated that they're not producing enough, not working hard enough, or not committed enough?

How much of your time is spent obsessing about how they just don't *get it*?

How often is your day completely ruined because you had to spend all your time putting out fires, listening to agent complaints and sob stories, and being an emotional counselor to everyone?

What percentage of your business life is spent being frustrated and stressed out about this stuff?

I've done business development seminars and sales coaching seminars all over the country, and the common response is 80%. That means that 80% of your business life is spent in utter misery. This is no way to live.

When you first got into the insurance industry, I doubt you said to yourself, "I can't wait to start spending 80% of the rest of my life in misery."

But that's where you are right now, right?

I've been there myself – frustrated and burned out.

But once I developed a better system, everything changed for the better. I went from virtually 0 to over $167,000 a month in renewal commissions within twenty-four months.

That's $167,000 per month, not per year. Now don't get all bent out of shape. I'm not telling you this to brag. I'm telling you this to illustrate that it's possible to make a hairline shift in your process and get a similar result. If I could do it, then you can do it too.

The 3 Key Elements Of A Great System

A great system has the power to establish and maintain the culture of an organization.

This is certainly not easy. If it were easy, everyone would do it flawlessly. In my journey as an agency owner, I was faced with several challenges in implementing my system.

The first challenge revolved around ramp-up time.

Generally speaking, trickle down process of implementing a system does not happen overnight. The challenge is, it takes time to make adjustments during a recalibration.

For me, the problem was that I didn't have time to allow for ramp-up time because I was going broke in my first year in this business. I needed to go straight from design to execution.

The good news was that I have always done my best work under an insurmountable amount of pressure.

As I thought through the design elements of creating a great system, there were three components that I knew were necessary if this was going to work.

Component #1: A Great System Must Be Simple.

Your system must be simple enough to *explain* and simple enough to *understand.*

A great system must not contain too many moving parts.

It must be completely void of any element that isn't absolutely necessary. It's got to be lean and mean.

Now don't misinterpret what I'm saying. I didn't say a great system was simple and easy to *develop.*

I said it must be simple and easy to *implement.*

That's the genius of a great system.

To illustrate this point, a friend of mine recently told me a story about Pablo Picasso.

Apparently, Picasso was sitting in a café, doodling on a cocktail napkin. The waitress saw him sketching and asked him if she could have his sketch.

Picasso said, "Sure, you may have this sketch for $50,000."

The waitress replied, "$50,000! Are you nuts? That only took you a few minutes to sketch."

Picasso replied, "My dear, this sketch did not just take me a few minutes to sketch. This sketch took me a lifetime."

What seems simple on the surface often times takes many years to create. Its development is extremely complex, and requires extensive recalibration in order to turn it into a masterpiece.

Now, I'm not likening myself to Picasso, but I will tell you that my business systems have taken many years to develop. It is the simplicity that allows for immediate implementation, immediate impact and immediate results.

One of my consulting clients was a billion dollar insurance carrier. I started doing business development consulting for them during the summer of 2009 on a variety of projects, one of which revolved around developing a new training program for their 6,000+ agents across the country.

In December of 2009, I finished developing some great new sales content to roll out at their annual kickoff meeting in January 2010.

It was December 2009, and I had just completed designing the new sales and marketing program for them. They wanted to run a test pilot using the program I developed for them prior to the January 2010 rollout.

Now, December is just about the worst month you could possibly rollout a new program simply due to the holiday season, but they were adamant about wanting to test my program prior to the January rollout, so I went along with it.

They decided to do two days of pilot testing, which is not even close to the amount of time needed to test most new programs. It's just not enough time to (1) ramp up the program, and (2) gather enough statistical data to quantify anything substantial.

In addition to these adverse conditions, they couldn't have picked two tougher days to test, and most new programs would fail under these circumstances.

My program wasn't like *most new programs*.

The first day was Friday, December 18th, which was the Friday before the week of Christmas.

The second day was Monday, December 21st, which was the week of Christmas.

They couldn't have picked a worse time to roll out my program. Despite these adverse conditions, we ran the test anyway.

I projected a 7% to 9% return during the first four to six weeks. Within these first two days, my pilot produced a 9.8% return.

That's the beauty of a great system. It requires virtually zero ramp-up time to implement, and produces immediate results.

In April 2010, the first quarter numbers came in.

After less than three months of my systems being implemented, their direct sales were up 53% over 2009's first quarter production.

Component #2: A Great System Is Specific.

The second component to a great system is that it must give people specific directives on what to do and how to do it.

Think about my story at the beginning of this book regarding my frustration at trying to assemble my son's baby bouncer with poor instructions.

I was confused and frustrated.

That's what happens to agents when they don't know exactly what to do or how to do it, especially when they're on straight-commission. They can only last so long being frustrated and confused before they quit.

Typically, that window is two to four weeks.

For some, they can't even last one day.

Now, this is where I've made huge mistakes in the past. I'd get so upset that people couldn't stick it out, and I'd label them as *weak*. I'd say things like, "If they only knew how hard I had to work," or, "Nobody ever gave me a system on a silver platter, and I figured it out on my own."

Have you ever found yourself saying things like this?

If the answer is yes, then you've felt the same frustration that I've experienced. This is the frustration of not having a *System-Driven Business*.

Yes, people should work harder.

Yes, people should be tougher.

The problem is that they won't work harder, they aren't tougher, and they most likely will never be able to figure it out on their own.

You need to accept this as the reality of life and design your agency to accommodate for this human deficiency.

In fact, you should just erase the word *should* from your vocabulary because there are a lot of things people *should* do but will never do.

Should you have to spoon-feed them to this degree?

Probably not.

Do you *have* to spoon-feed them to this degree?

Only if you want to be successful.

In my organization, every word that comes out of my people's mouths is coached.

The content is coached.

The speech inflection is coached.

The speech rhythm is coached.

The voice volume is coached.

Everything is coached.

I teach my people why my method of communication works, what my philosophy behind each scripted word is, and how each script was engineered.

I teach them the subconscious interpretation of each subtle linguistic pattern we use and why people respond the way they do.

You see, if you have a very specific method of communication, operation, and execution, and your people understand how to execute using your system, you've got a *System-Driven* sales process.

Once you have this, you've got a *machine*.

Your people will love you because they know your system is what's making them successful, and that without you and your system, they'd make less money on their own.

Now you're holding all the cards.

Your people will never experience the frustration of not knowing exactly what to do. They won't have that paralysis by analysis moment where they freeze up due to confusion and lack of clarity.

This is why it's so important to have a clearly defined *Standard Operating Procedure (SOP)*.

This is a meticulously *taught* method of how to prospect, close, and retain business – a trained set of rules that everyone in your organization must adhere to.

For example, in my organization, we never leave a proposal behind without a signed commitment from the client to do business with us.

Never.

Why?

Because we know that at least 30% of the prospects we meet with are going to lie to us.

They're going to lead us to believe that they're legitimately interested in doing business with us, when all along, they were planning to take our ideas back to their broker and cut us out of the deal.

I hate to admit it, but I do the same thing as a consumer.

I'll spend an hour with a sales guy at retail store, asking him tons of questions about a TV, and then I'll go buy it online for a cheaper price.

That's why you never want to leave a proposal behind with a prospect unless they give you a commitment to do business with you by signing a contract.

The only time leaving a proposal behind makes sense is if your competition cannot replicate it. If you have a proprietary product or service, leaving a proposal behind can reinforce your expertise and dominance in the space.

But if you're just brokering a product, and you leave your proposal behind, all you did was demonstrate that you are a commodity.

This is just one example of several rules of engagement that I teach my agents to follow. This is part of our *Standard Operating Procedure (SOP)*.

Your *SOP* must be very specific.

Once everyone knows the rules, it's an easy process to execute because everyone knows exactly what to do, how to do it, and why we do it in this manner.

When I do business development consulting for other insurance agencies, one of the first things I do is have them tell me what their *SOP* is.

In other words, I ask them to explain the process they go through from generating a prospect, to procuring the sale, to retaining the client. In most cases, they don't have a premeditated process.

That's what they hire me for. I create a simple, easy to follow method of operation so that all of their agents are marching to the same beat of the same drum.

When I create an *SOP* for these types of agencies, I make sure that every person in their organization knows exactly what to do in every scenario imaginable.

I've had so many agency owners tell me how amazed they were at how fast their agents adopted and implemented my systems, and how quickly they started getting results.

In my opinion, a truly great system will yield you results within the first week, and sometimes, within the first day.

Component #3: A Great System Has Proof of Concept.

The third component of a great system is that it must have *Proof of Concept*. I can't stand these wannabe, so-called *sales trainers* that teach things that they've never successfully done themselves.

Even worse, I've seen training programs that teach people to do things that haven't been statistically proven to work over time.

When I question these sales trainers about the legitimacy of their training programs, they say things like, "This *should* work."

My response is always, "If you're so confident, then test it for thirty to sixty days, and once you have the proof, then roll it out to everyone."

This usually infuriates them because they know they don't fully believe in their program. If they did, they'd run a pilot and prove it.

I only teach things that have been statistically proven through vigorous testing and have produced quantifiable results.

The only thing that matters is the truth – what has been proven to work over time. I don't base my teachings on opinions and mere philosophies. I base them on proven, quantifiable statistics.

I base them on the truth.

If the foundation of a teaching is merely based on someone's opinion, then it's complete garbage.

On a recent project, a voluntary benefits insurance carrier contracted me to revamp, redesign, and rebrand their entire sales approach.

They told me that they wanted me to *change the culture* of the company, which is a big undertaking, to say the least.

When I started designing an *SOP* for them, I wrote a cold-calling script. I also designed a video-embedded *PowerPoint* to be used on a first appointment with a prospect.

I designed this program to be completely dummy-proof.

The first push back I got was from the veterans in the company that told me that they just weren't a cold-calling culture.

I guess they didn't get the memo that my job was to change the entire culture of the organization *to* a cold-calling culture.

They said, "Darren, it's obviously worked for you, but we sell voluntary benefits. Your organization sells major medical. It's different."

Yeah, whatever.

So we rolled this out in Newport Beach, California, at their territory office, and we got the exact results that I expected.

The next objection was that it was a *Southern California thing* and that it wouldn't work in the *Midwest*.

So we did it again in Chicago and actually got better results than we did in Newport Beach, California.

They balked, "Yeah Darren, but those are two *big-city* markets. This wouldn't work in a small rural market."

So we did it again in Little Rock, Arkansas. Same results.

Tulsa, Oklahoma. Same results.

Charlotte, North Carolina. Same results.

Boston, Massachusetts. Same results.

Houston, Texas. Same results.

Dublin, Ohio. Same results.

Las Vegas, Nevada. Same results.

When you have a truly great system, it works in *any* market with *any* sales organization, as long as they follow the protocol and execute the system in its entirety – emphasis on *entirety*.

Only running parts of the system will not work.

It's like baking a cake and only using part of the recipe. Leave out one or two key ingredients – like sugar and flour – and you will not produce a cake. You'll produce a disgusting blob of goo that is anything but a cake.

Great systems contain concepts that work regardless of the industry because they're based on understanding human psychology, human behavioral patterns, and the human subconscious mind.

The key to everything I'm talking about is systematizing every single process within your agency. When your people know exactly what to do and how to do it, you have a *System-Driven Business*.

If you're an agency owner, the ultimate goal is to build an agency filled with successful producers that can rely on the *system* to make things happen, not *you*. Do this, and you won't have to baby sit your producers 24/7. You won't have to touch every transaction that takes place in your agency.

If you have to touch every single actionable item that goes through your agency, then you don't have a *business*. You have a *job*, and guess who your boss is. Your agents.

You'll be overworked, overly stressed out, and eventually, you're going to get burned out.

Perhaps you're there right now.

The reality is, you can't be everything to everyone 100% of the time, but the right system can.

Liberate yourself, and stop carrying the burden of your entire team on your back.

CHAPTER 5

WHY EVERYONE HATES SCRIPTS

Most people that I work with are initially very resistant to the idea of using sales scripts.

I don't blame them because most scripts suck.

I've read tons of sales scripts, and let me tell you, most of them are just awful. They sound unnatural, disingenuous and inauthentic.

A great script is just the opposite.

A great script sounds chit-chatty, feels slightly nonchalant, and always has an offer that is just too compelling to dismiss.

A great script makes the prospect say, "Wow, I've never heard of that before. Tell me more."

When I create a script, I'm hitting several subconscious triggers that make the prospect practically beg for the appointment, and I teach why each element works from a neurolinguistics perspective.

Many veterans in the insurance business will tell me, "I don't need a script. I've been doing this for twenty-five years, and I don't want to sound *unnatural*."

It never ceases to amaze me that people's egos will get in the way of their own success.

These people think they're *above* using a script.

Hey, Robert DeNiro uses a script, and the last time I checked, his 1099 was bigger than both of ours combined. So if Robert DeNiro isn't above using a script, then neither are you.

There are two components of a successful script:
1. The content.
2. The delivery.

For example, have you ever seen the movie *Pride and Prejudice*? Women love this movie. I've probably seen this movie with my wife over a dozen times.

She absolutely loves this movie.

Women all say, "Mr. Darcy is so romantic."

Listen, honey, Mr. Darcy is a character played by an actor.

It's not him. He's not romantic. He's just reading a script.

Ladies, aren't you just crushed at hearing these words?

He's just reciting a script, but he's got you crying your eyeballs out.

Why?

Because he's got a great script, and he's damn good at delivering it.

This combination – the script content and the delivery by the actor – has created strong emotions within you.

That's what a great movie script does, and that's also what a great sales script does. They both create a specific desired emotional response.

Great actors have been known to do intensive research on their roles, learning how their character thinks, talks, and walks. They seek to fully understand the mindset of their characters, and learn to master their every little idiosyncrasy.

But it's the screenwriters – the authors of the scripts – that are the master visionaries of creating and weaving together the fabric of the story.

And then the director coaches the actor through the process of bringing the right energy into the scene to make it come alive.

As an agency owner, you have to take on the role of both the screenwriter and the director. You have to be *Martin Scorsese* in order to produce a bunch of *Robert DeNiros*.

You also have to be the *studio executive* and the *investor* who is financing the entire operation too. I know, it's a lot to take on.

What Makes a Great Script a *Great Script*?

There are several stages of a great script.

The first stage sets the *emotional state*.

When you're cold-calling, the prospect is in a particular emotional state when they answer your phone call.

Do you think the prospect is in an emotional state of curiosity, intrigue, and excitement?

Of course not.

They're in an emotional state of annoyance, skepticism, and disinterest. When you call a business owner or a decision maker on the phone, you have about a 95% chance that you're interrupting them right in the middle of doing something important and urgent.

Business owners and decision makers are generally busy.

They're not kicking back in their office watching TV and eating bon-bons all day.

They're working, and they're probably stressed out.

By definition, you're interrupting them.

Their initial emotional state is not one of receptivity, so the script must break them out of their *current* emotional state in order to get them into the *proper* emotional state.

So how do you do this?

You do this by using the proper *Emotional State Breaking Language*. One of the best emotional state breaking lines is, "I'm glad I got a hold of you." This creates positive expectation on a subconscious level.

If I was to call you up in the middle of your day and say, "Oh, man! I'm glad I got a hold of you," your ears would perk up, and you'd be anticipating either good news or important news.

Either way, your emotional state would be one of receptivity.

We use this same technique when cold-call prospecting. It makes the prospect subconsciously say, "Really! Why?"

This doesn't happen at the conscious level, only at the subconscious level.

This is much better than starting the phone call off with, "Hi, this is John from XYZ corporation. How are you?"

Do you really think he thinks you actually care about how his day is going?

You're not fooling anyone, plus it comes off as disingenuous.

That's why I hate this suck-up approach. If it worked, I still wouldn't like it because I abhor the suck-up approach, but I'd have to say, "Okay, I guess sucking up works."

But the truth is, it doesn't work.

The key is to break them out of their emotional state and then hit them with a compelling offer that they can't ignore or dismiss. They may not initially say *yes*, but they won't initially say *no*, either.

The offer must be intriguing enough for them to *not interrupt* you or hang up the phone before you get your whole message out.

This process I'm about to explain to you is what I call *BIT Communication.*

BIT Communication

BIT is an acronym for *Benefit, Inside Story, Testimonial.*

The *Benefit* tells them what they're going to get out of doing business with you. Typically, if the benefit presented is really good for them, the most common objection is that it sounds too good to be true.

Since we already know this, our goal is to immediately tell them the *Inside Story.*

The *Inside Story* is the behind-the-scenes story that explains why the *Benefit* exists. It validates the legitimacy of the our proposition.

For example, if the *Benefit* is a monetary savings, the *Inside Story* might revolve around a new law that just passed, or a change in legislature.

Inside Stories are most powerful when they revolve around something new. People love *new*.

In marketing, the three most powerful words that command the strongest knee-jerk reactions are:

1. Free
2. Sex
3. New

Now, in the insurance world, you can't give away free insurance. It's illegal.

I highly recommend that you don't give away the second one. It's also illegal in some states.

So, we're left with the third one.

New.

When the new body style of a car comes out, everyone wants the *new* version. The old body style might be better than the new one, but it doesn't matter. People still want the new one.

Here's another example.

I once purchased a video camera. Within a couple of weeks, it died on me, so I took it back to the store I bought it from.

Fortunately, it was under warranty, so they told me they'd replace it with the same one.

The sales guy starts entering my information into the system to process the exchange, and then he says, "Well, your model has been discontinued, and we don't have any more of your models in stock."

I said, "Okay, I'll take the new model." I was actually pretty excited. I liked the idea of getting the *new* model.

The sales guy said, "The only problem is that we're not getting the new models until next week's shipment."

I said, "Well I've got a speaking engagement tomorrow, and I need a video camera right now."

So the sales guy told me, "Hold on a second. Let me do a search to see if another one of our stores has any in stock."

Then he says, "Ah-ha! The Costa Mesa store has two in stock. I'll call them right now and tell them to hold one for you."

I said, "Perfect! That's the *new* model, right?"

"No," he said, "it's the old one."

"The old one? Man, I don't want the old, discontinued, out-of-date, obsolete one. I want the *new* one."

Now think about this.

I was perfectly happy with my video camera before it broke. It was great. All of a sudden, as soon as I learned that there was a *new* version, I hated my video camera.

I hadn't even seen the new one yet. Maybe the new one sucked. It didn't matter.

I still wanted the new one.

That's the way people are.

Human beings are always intrigued by new things.

Most people want to at least find out what's *new* in the marketplace, just to find out if there's something better than their current version.

The word *new* also implies *relevance*.

People are generally resistant to change their past decisions, but they are actually very open to making *new* decisions based on *new* information.

After we've communicated that something new exists, we hit them with a *Testimonial*. We'll show them a real-life example of a client that received this *Benefit*, and why it solved a problem that they didn't even know they had.

This creates *positive jealousy*.

The prospect becomes ticked off that someone else has something better than them, which makes them want us to deliver the same *Benefit* to them.

At this point, they want to hear more about our offering than we want to share it with them.

This is where the *Role Reversal* begins.

Role Reversal

In the dating world, typically, women have all the power.

Why?

Because typically, the man is the one pursuing the woman. By definition, the woman has the power simply because she has the ability to reject the man's proposal.

The man is in the position of weakness because he is outwardly admitting that he wants the woman more than the woman wants him.

The woman has the upper hand in this dynamic because she has walk-away power, and the man does not.

As far as optics go, the man is in a position of weakness and desperation, and there is nothing more repulsive to a woman than a desperate man.

In sales, you will often times find yourself in the exact same position as the desperate man, there is nothing more repulsive to a prospect than a desperate sales rep.

They can smell the desperation seeping out of your pores.

What you need to do is reverse the roles.

You need to create *Walk Away Power*.

The question is, "How do you do this?"

It starts with creating *Positive Jealousy*.

You need to communicate to the prospect that they might be getting a bad deal and that you're offering a better deal.

That's the *Benefit*.

You then need to communicate that you have top-secret, behind-the-scenes information, not known to the general public and that this information is the reason why this *Benefit* exists.

That's the *Inside Story*.

Then, you hit them with a real-life story of one of your clients that got that exact same benefit, and you reinforce to them that you're the only one that can deliver this product, service, or strategy.

That's the *Testimonial*.

So, you've got them intrigued, curious, and jealous.

Once you create this *Positive Jealousy* – meaning that the prospect is envious of your client and the results you were able to produce for them – you have all the power.

They want the *Benefit* more than you want them as a client.

Of course you want them as a client too, but their desire to have the benefit is stronger than your *need* to close them.

That's why I hate the term *closing* a prospect.

It makes is sound like you *forced* them – or even worse, *tricked* them – into signing on the dotted line. You should be *serving* the client, not *closing* the client.

Creating *Positive Jealousy* is not a manipulative thing.

It's the art of clearly communicating to the prospective client what the actual benefit of your product or service is, and there is no better way to do that than by showing them a real life example of someone that has benefitted from your proposed solution.

Other than having one of your clients tell them how much they love your product or service, showing your prospect a case study is the next best thing.

Jealousy is one of the most powerful human emotions. Use it in a positive way in sales and you'll triple the amount of business you generate.

All you have to do now is set the appointment.

As you probably already know, booking the appointment is not so easy unless you have a script with great sales language.

The Appointment Booking Script

The appointment booking script must have a strong *call-to-action*. You don't want to blow it here, or all of your efforts will have been in vain.

Don't ask, "What I'd like to do is set up a meeting with you."

First of all, no one cares what *you* would like to do.

They only care about what *they* would like to do.

And don't ask for permission either. It makes you sound desperate.

So don't tell them what *you'd* like to do, and don't ask them to grant you permission either.

Instead, make a *Suggestive Proposition*.

Wrap up your prospecting call by saying, "What probably makes the most sense is to get together and see if there's a fit," or, "Let's just see if there's a good fit; it'll only take about fifteen minutes."

Suggestive Propositions are strong, but not overbearing.

They just make good sense, and that's really what you're trying to accomplish with a prospect. You want them to say in their subconscious mind, "What the heck, I'll meet with you to see what whatcha got."

Lastly, you want to dictate the day and time of the appointment.

Don't ask, "So what does your schedule look like?"

This is just plain weak and desperate. It implies that you have nothing else going on, which means you are not *in-demand*, and if you're not *in-demand*, then you must not have anything of value.

It's like a guy asking a girl out, and when she says she's busy, and he says, "What about next weekend... or the weekend after that... or the weekend after that... because I've got nothing else going on and I'm desperate and nobody else wants me either."

What you want to say is, "Let me check my schedule here... I have an opening on Thursday at 10 o'clock... how does that work for you?"

You know *who else does this?*

Doctors' offices.

When you call a doctor's office to request your annual check-up, they don't ask you what *your* schedule looks like.

They tell you when the doctor's next available opening is, and you eagerly jump at the opportunity and say, "I'll take it!"

Why?

Because you're afraid of losing that appointment slot. You know they're busy and in-demand, so you conform to whatever their schedule is.

That's what you want the prospect to do with you, and quite frankly, they *should*. If you have something of great value, they will do whatever it takes to be the beneficiary of your program.

Now the roles have been reversed, and they are chasing you – not the other way around. They should be more excited about meeting with you than you are with them.

Once you accomplish this, you're in a whole different league. You used to be perceived as the *Desperate Guy in the Bar*.

Instead, now you're *Brad Pitt*.

That's what a great script does. It puts you in-demand and in control, which puts you in a different league.

What I've Learned Over The Last 10 Years About Scripts

There are some universal truths that never change over time. Human beings have wanted the same things since the very beginning of time.

We want to feel important.

We want to feel smart.

We want to feel special.

When I originally wrote the *First Edition* of this book ten years ago, I had mapped out a very delineated sales process that revolved around neuro-linguistic programming.

Ten years later, I am still a huge proponent of using scripts.

A great script is better than the best freestyle performance from the most talented salesperson.

Extremely talented salespeople will continue to disagree with me on this issue. In a face-to-face interaction, there are several intangible strengths that a *talented* salesperson brings to the table.

Their aura of confidence certainly helps.

If they are polished in appearance and have a level of professionalism that screams, "I am the expert in my field," that certainly helps too.

If they put out the right vibe and exude positive energy, that is definitely a plus. Some of these talents can be learned through extensive coaching, but some of them are just part of a person's DNA and cannot be taught.

These unique individuals have a *star quality* that can't be quantified or duplicated. Now, some of these qualities can be translated over the phone and in a webinar environment, but some of them cannot.

Without the ability to fully capitalize on your *star quality* due to the way a webinar video dilutes the magic, you need to maximize the other attributes of your presentation.

One way to do this is to remove as many potential distractions from your presentation as possible, which includes keeping your content consistent, as well as your delivery. Scripts greatly assist in this process.

I've listened to recordings of conference call presentations and webinar presentations that I've done over the years – with and without scripts – and my articulation of complex concepts is just not as clean and concise as webinars where I've used a script.

The way to understand the value of a great script is to first agree that if you compare one way of articulating something to another way of articulating the exact same thing, one of those two versions is better.

One version is easier to understand and provides more clarity than the other version.

If this is true (which it is), then why wouldn't you want your client to hear your *best version* every single time?

If we're going to agree that we want to maximize our results, then we should do everything within our power to create the very best client experience possible, which includes how we deliver our message.

If the client gets distracted for just one moment during your pitch, you will have lost any momentum you may have created. If you say one little thing that gets interpreted as being confusing or uncertain, the prospect will withdraw.

When selling over the phone remotely, the stakes are even higher. They can't connect with you by looking into your eyes. If you're using your video meeting capability, perhaps they can see your face, but it's in a one-inch by one-inch box on their computer screen. Again, it's just not the same as being in-person.

On top of that, there is a 99% chance that as you're presenting, they're simultaneously checking emails, browsing social media, and not giving you 100% of their undivided attention.

But if your content is incredibly compelling, and your delivery is impeccable, you have the ability to fully captivate their attention on a screenshare meeting.

When we began to transition to a more life insurance-focused model with the launch of *DaVinci Financial*, it was necessary to make our *PowerPoint* presentations and scripts even more engaging.

After all, life insurance isn't the sexiest product around, at least not to the unsuspecting prospect.

We had to explain the difference between *term insurance* and *permanent insurance*, how certain policies build *cash value*, how IRC Section 7702 benefits them from a tax standpoint, and an array of other first-exposure concepts.

We were essentially *teachers*.

Our message had to be very clear and concise. Our articulation of these relatively complex concepts needed to be succinct, easy to understand, and quick to adopt. It also needed to be fully transparent and detailed for believability and credibility purposes, but not so overly-detailed that it confused the heck out of the prospect.

This is a fine balance – the balance of being detailed enough to fulfill our fiduciary responsibility to the client, but not so detailed that it spoke above their intellectual capacity– and very few agents in the financial services industry have mastered this skill.

My script gave me quality control over the message my agents were delivering to the clients. In addition, virtual meetings allowed me to sit right next to my agents to ensure our clients were receiving the proper content in the communication style I desired.

In fact, I could even pipe in remotely.

However, the benefit of a great script is not limited to agent quality control and compliance monitoring.

Remember, I even use scripts myself when doing presentations, because the script is the tightest, most succinct possible way of articulating the message I want to articulate.

Why would I want to deliver my *second-best* when I have already taken the time to construct the perfect, premeditated script?

Of course they should *feel* natural and not like a rehearsed pitch delivered by a news anchor reading off a teleprompter. A great script will always sound *natural*.

As much as my presentations are script-based, I'm also prepared to pivot and elaborate on a topic if asked to.

Hence, I have a several pre-authored responses to questions I know will come up. I have the framework of bullet points prepared to handle everything I may have to cover if the conversation turns into a more interactive dialogue, with key go-to snippets that are scripted and recited verbatim.

You can't be a *Ron Burgundy* (from the movie *Anchorman*) and not be able to carry on a conversation that isn't in the exact chronological order of the paragraphs on your script.

That being said, you should absolutely have bullet points on your *cheat sheet* that you can reference, with key phrases that can transition you back onto the script content without sounding like a robot.

That's actually one of the advantages you have when running virtual sales calls using a screenshare program. You can use a *cheat sheet* during your call without the prospect even knowing.

For highly-skilled sales experts that have memorized the script and can brilliantly spit out the script and make it sound like they're just chatting freestyle, the script is their back-up content.

It's like wearing a belt AND suspenders.

Your talent is the *belt*. The script is your *suspenders*.

For new agents, they don't have a belt yet, so they'd better use the suspenders you provide them with.

But even for elite sales professionals, every once in a while, their *belt* fails. They'll get distracted or have a bad day from time to time, albeit a rare occasion. This is where having a brilliant script comes in.

It requires discipline to have that level of consistency on a day-to-day basis, and even for me, using a script can feel boring and monotonous at times.

But I challenge you to record one of your calls unscripted, and compare it to a recording of one of your scripted calls.

You will be shocked at how much stronger you sound when scripted.

CHAPTER 6

PRESENTING V. CREATING AN EXPERIENCE

I absolutely hate the term *sales presentation*, just like I hate the terms *closer* and *recruiter*.

Think about it.

Do you want to sit through a *sales presentation*?

I don't either.

It just sounds boring, and in most cases, sales presentations *are* indeed boring.

A *presentation* doesn't seek to connect or communicate.

Brochures, graphs, pie charts and all of that *presentation fluff* is meaningless if your message doesn't connect or resonate with the prospect.

Don't do *sales presentations*.

Instead, create an *experience* for the prospect – a unique, compelling experience that makes it clear to them that you are the only one they should be doing business with, and no one else.

How do you do this?

It all starts the minute you walk into their office to greet them, and most sales reps blow it right from the start.

They *thank* the prospect for their time.

Never Thank the Prospect for Their Time

This is one of the biggest mistakes people in sales make.

The first thing they do when they walk into an appointment is say, "Thank you for taking the time to meet with me today."

This is completely illogical.

This is what most amateurs do.

The reason this is an illogical greeting is that when you say, "Thank you for your time," it implies that the prospect is somehow doing you a favor by meeting with you.

The prospect did not do you a *favor* by meeting with you.

If you end up doing the deal with the prospect, who's getting the better end of the deal?

In other words, when you look at the value the prospect is about to receive by working with you – whether it be a dollar savings, greater convenience, etc. – versus the value you receive (commission amount), who's getting the better deal?

If you're getting a better deal than the prospect is getting – meaning you're making more commission than the client is receiving in value – then you screwed them.

The client should always get the better end of the deal.

If you're truly looking to serve the client properly and ethically, the client should always get more value from doing business with you in comparison to what you're personally making in commissions.

By thanking them for their time, you're establishing the wrong type of relationship dynamic from the very beginning..

When you meet with your doctor, does he thank you for taking the time to come into his office?

Of course not.

Sure, he makes money for his medical evaluation of your health, but you're the one that's getting the real value.

It's the same thing with the service you provide to your clients. If you just look at it in simple terms, whoever got the better end of the deal should thank the one that went above and beyond what would normally be expected.

If you take me out to dinner, then *I* should thank *you*.

If I take you out to dinner, then *you* should thank *me*.

It's pretty simple.

But in sales, most sales reps don't ever stop to consider the underlying message they're communicating when they thank a prospect or a client for their time.

Now, I'm not saying to be rude.

Not at all.

What I'm suggesting is that you must change your message from, "Thank you for your time today" to "I'm really glad we could get together today. I think we're going to be able to help you guys out."

It's just as friendly, but what the prospect subconsciously hears is that:

1. You're there to help them.
2. You're glad to do it.

...versus, when you thank them for their time, they hear:

1. I appreciate the opportunity for me make money off you.
2. I'm definitely going to make money off you.

And the best part is that when you tell them you think you're going to be able to help them out, guess what the prospect will say in return.

They'll say, "That would be great. Thank you."

Now you can say, "You're very welcome."

Isn't it interesting how something so seemingly minor can make such a dramatic difference in the way you are perceived by the prospect?

They will have a greater level of respect and appreciation for what you do, which is exactly what you want.

I know this concept of *not thanking* people for their time seems a bit counterintuitive, and it probably makes you feel a little uncomfortable because this is what you've become accustomed to doing for so long.

If you think it's difficult for you to feel comfortable with this new line of thinking and communicating, it was even harder for me to get comfortable with due to my Japanese heritage and the way I was raised.

For example, in the Japanese culture, when you go to someone's home, you must bring a gift as a token of appreciation for being an invited guest.

Now, when they come and visit you at your home, they also have to bring you a gift as a token of appreciation for being your invited guest, but they will feel compelled to out-gift you. Their gift must be greater than the gift you gave them.

Now you're screwed because if you get invited back to their home, you have to out-gift them. It becomes a vicious cycle of out-gifting the other, and before you know it, you're practically trading Ferraris.

I tell you this to illustrate just how different the concept of *not thanking* a prospect is, compared to how I was raised.

I admire and appreciate culture, but when culture stands in the way of me establishing the level of respect I demand in a relationship, I have a problem with culture.

So as uncomfortable as this communication strategy may make you feel initially, just change the phraseology you use, and watch how much your clients' perception of you and the value of your services changes for the better.

Again, just tell them that you're excited about what you can do for them, and quite frankly, you *should* be excited and passionate about what you do.

Just make sure you communicate that your excitement is based on the benefit you're delivering to the client, not your commission check.

The Goal of the First Appointment

Whether the first appointment be face-to-face or via conference call and screenshare, the goal is for the prospect to say,

"Wow, this is cool. I've never seen anything like this before. If you can really deliver what you say you can, I'm in."

A *sales presentation* doesn't elicit this kind of response.

In order to elicit the response you're looking for, you have to create a *unique experience* for the prospect, which involves surfacing certain emotions within the prospect within a very short amount of time, which is a huge task.

In addition, you have two distinct disadvantages compared to the incumbent broker:

1. Familiarity.
2. Longevity of relationship.

There's no way you're going to establish more credibility and trust with the prospect in a sixty-minute meeting than the other guy has established over several years. It's impossible.

So don't try to build trust and rapport, because you're destined to lose that battle.

Instead, get them to *distrust* their current broker.

How do you do this?

Just uncover the truth.

Uncovering the Truth

Here's an example of how to uncover the truth.

A guy meets a girl in a bar. The girl has a boyfriend. She's been with her boyfriend for five years. She's *in love* with her boyfriend.

There's no way the new guy is going to make this girl fall in love with him *more* than she already is with her current boyfriend, especially within a sixty-minute bar chat.

There's no way she's going to trust this new guy over her current boyfriend because trust takes a long time to build.

But how long does it take to *break* trust?

About thirty seconds.

If this new guy shows the girl digital pictures of her so-called boyfriend snuggled up in a dark corner of a restaurant with some hot blonde chick on a night where he was supposed to be hanging out with the boys, trust has been broken within a matter of seconds.

Who's she going to trust more now?

The new guy hasn't established *any* trust yet – he's neutral – however he is not *distrusted* the way the cheating boyfriend is.

Comparatively speaking, *no trust* is better than *distrust*.

The point is, you don't need to win trust with a prospect on this first-meet. If you can get the prospect to *distrust* the incumbent, you will win by default.

Plus it's easier to do.

I call this process the *Incumbent Broker Character Assassination*.

The Incumbent Broker Character Assassination

Your goal should be to assassinate the character and integrity of their current broker, and in most cases, it isn't hard to do.

I made the above statement in my original *First Edition* of this book ten years ago. Here I am, ten years older and ten years wiser, and I slightly cringe at this statement when viewed as a stand-alone statement. Allow me to give this statement some context.

It is 100% appropriate to assassinate the character of the incumbent if the solution they provided is crap. In my personal experience, whether it is the group health insurance industry, or the P&C industry, or the life insurance industry, or the investment industry, the majority of cases I've personally worked on have been rescue missions.

Very rare is it to see a well-executed solution in any of these industries. Most clients were sold something they didn't completely understand by a broker that didn't completely understand what they sold.

However if the client is in a good position that I cannot improve, I will not try to get the client to move for my own benefit.

This is called *churning* and I am against it. Any move away from a current strategy into a new one has to make sense for the client.

It has to be an appropriate and *suitable* switch. That being said, in most cases, I can drastically improve their situation.

Most brokers are complacent, lazy, and incompetent, so all you need to do is uncover the areas where the broker has underperformed for the client.

For example, ask the client why they think their broker didn't show them the new, creative ways to save money that you're showing them.

There are only two possible answers.

1. They didn't know these options existed, which means their broker is incompetent compared to us.
2. The broker knew these options existed, but elected to sell the client a vanilla off-the-shelf policy, which means their broker is lazy.

So which one are they, incompetent or lazy?

Either way, the client realizes they've been getting a crappy deal, and they no longer trust their broker. If you're the one that exposed all of these wrongdoings, you will win the comparative *trust battle* against the incumbent broker.

Here are a few simple questions to use when wrapping up a first-meet with a prospective client:

1. Has anyone ever showed you these strategies before?
2. Why do you think your current broker never showed you this?
3. Is there anything they're offering you now that you're afraid of losing?
4. Is there anything about our program you don't like or don't think is appropriate for you right now?
5. Can you think of any reason why you wouldn't want to switch brokers and start getting these benefits?

This simple series of questions allows us to acquire new clients before we even ask for a census, run numbers, or deliver a proposal.

You want to win over clients based on concepts and unique value-added services, not rates and benefits. Selling on price sucks.

Let's talk very briefly about selling on price.

If you're trying to compete showing apples-to-apples cost comparisons on a spreadsheet – products that are commodities that any broker can offer – then you're easily dispensable.

Anyone can generate a quote or a proposal.

There's nothing special or compelling about that.

You've got to show them something unique.

Now, that being said, you can show them a unique strategy that also just so happens to save them money, but the emphasis must be on the unique strategy, not the cost savings.

Sure, they may sign the deal over to you because the strategy saved them money, but this is different than selling on price alone.

This is showing them a unique strategy that they've never seen before – again, emphasis on unique.

A lot of agents get this confused.

The untrained eye will see my selling strategy and say, "Darren, all of your agents sell on price."

To the untrained amateur eye, I can see how they could misinterpret our process because the focus appeared to be on the cost savings.

However, what the amateur eye is not seeing is that our selling process was actually not focused cost savings, but rather the unique *strategy* that generated the cost savings.

There is a big difference.

All of our so-called *cost savings strategies* are uniquely packaged, articulated and branded. They are all unique propositions that the prospect has never seen before, which is why they're signing the deal over to us, often times without even seeing a formal quote or proposal yet.

You've got to have a *Unique Selling Proposition (USP)*.

A great *USP* answers the question, "Why should someone do business with you and only you? What can they get from you that they cannot get from anybody else?"

Once you answer this question, you have a *USP*.

Now, you are in a position of ultimate power.

USPs are not cool, interesting, or different.

They are unique – one-of-a-kind.

Once you establish the fact that the prospect wants what you have and they perceive that they can't get it from anyone else, you have accomplished the *role reversal* we talked about earlier.

The two easiest ways to create that unique experience we talked about earlier are:
1. Ask them questions they don't know the answers to.
2. Show them things they've never seen before.

If you do these two simple things, you will have established yourself as the undisputed expert in the room. They will defer to you now because they realize two things:
1. You know something that they don't.
2. The incumbent broker didn't know how to do it either.

Case Studies

Another key to creating a unique experience for the prospect on a first meeting is showing them case studies – examples of real clients you've worked with that have gotten real results using the exact same strategies that you're proposing.

Case studies are huge because they demonstrate *Proof of Concept*. Case studies are undeniable.

Prospects can't look at a case study and say, "This is too good to be true."

It is true, and it's staring at them right in the face.

The only objection they could have at this point is, "Yeah, but I just don't know if this would work for *my* unique situation."

That's a great reaction because all you have to say at that point is, "Well, let's find out and run the numbers for you."

This proposition drives the next step.

Toward the end of the meeting – once you've dazzled them with all of these great ideas, strategies, programs, and case studies to back up your claims – they'll want you to run the numbers.

At this point, immediately book the follow-up meeting, which they should be begging for by now.

Once you book the follow up meeting, you've given them something that you know they want – the chance to see if you can really help them or not.

You know you have their attention because if you didn't, they wouldn't have booked the second appointment with you.

Now you have *leverage*.

What does this mean?

It means that you have the power to take away that which you have given to them if they don't want to play the game by your rules.

You now have the power to dictate the next step.

Requiring them to sign a *Broker Exclusivity Letter* or a *Letter of Intent* on a first-meet might seem like an audacious request, but if you know you have what they want, it's not an unreasonable expectation.

If you have the guts to require that they sign a *Broker of Record Letter* at this point, you call the shots. You have ultimate leverage because you have walk-away power.

You have walk-away power now because the prospect wants the opportunity to work with you more than you want to work with them. You are now *Brad Pitt*, and everyone wants you.

What I've Learned About This Positioning 10 Years Later

In the last ten years, nothing has changed in this regard.

Not one thing.

My system and sales content has evolved and continues to improve over time, but the core principles still apply.

First, we show the client something they've never seen before.

Then we show them the flaw in their current set up (if one indeed exists).

Then we articulate our *USP*.

Then show them case studies.

And then we wrap with our requirement based on our rules of engagement, or we walk away.

How's that for clarity?

Obviously, the specifics will vary from industry to industry, and from line of insurance to line of insurance (assuming you're in the insurance business).

In any case, I will give you the *framework*, but you've got to do the *homework* in developing your own system.

The first thing you need to do is identify what everyone else (your competitors) are doing, and commit to NOT do that.

Here are some examples of what we did with some of my companies. Because each one of these companies specializes in a different line of insurance, I will explain how I developed a different *USP* for each company.

Lionsmark Capital

In *Lionsmark Capital* (my premium financing firm), our unique client experience started with us developing our own software to show the client how the cash value of life insurance policy actually works.

We transparently show the client things that no other agent would ever show them – things like policy charges, hidden fees, how the net index credit is calculated, how the product would perform in adverse scenarios – and we transparently focus on the worst case scenario, not the best case scenario.

Our competitors sell based on illustrating a *rainbows and unicorns* scenario, so we decided to do the opposite. We figured out that some of the biggest concerns that clients had revolved around risk – what happens if the market doesn't perform, or borrowing rates become hyper-inflated, or carriers' floors and caps change, or lenders' collateral requirements change.

We model the most adverse conditions that could possibly exist, all happening concurrently. This is a completely unrealistic scenario, but we realized that nobody had the confidence in their programs to show these adverse scenarios, which gave us the opportunity to fill this void. To this day, none of our competitors have the software to model this the way we do.

We also don't try to sell the prospect on how great the concept of premium financing is, let alone how great *our* unique premium financing model is.

Instead, we show them a comparative analysis of their other investment alternatives – relative to our platform – and we focus on this comparison during times of poor market performance and adverse volatility.

None of our competitors were doing this either, and even today at the time of me writing this *Second Edition* of this book three years after we started doing this, still none of our competitors are doing this.

So here is our framework of our *Playbook*:

1. Most premium financing firms show illustrations with static annual returns and low borrowing rates.

2. The problem with this is if the borrowing rates increase and the index doesn't perform well in the beginning, the LTV is too far upside down, and the client is going to get hit with a large collateral call. No one is showing the client what would happen if market volatility and a spike in borrowing rates cause a negative arbitrage effect.

3. What makes us different is we are the only premium financing firm that can model policy index volatility, a poor sequence of returns, and fluctuating borrowing rates simultaneously. Due to our unique relationships with our lenders and carrier partners, we can get our clients access to loan programs and policy designs that none of our competitors can compete with.
4. In our programs, the clients do not need to post outside collateral, and though the standard minimum net worth requirement is $5 million, we can get clients access to our programs with an income of $200,000 and a net worth of only $500,000.
5. Our competitors can't offer this because their programs are risky, over-leveraged, and irresponsibly overly-aggressive.
6. I will then show them a case study using one of our clients that used our program, and explicitly articulate the difference in outcome compared to:
    a. A non-financed policy.
    b. A financed policy designed by our competitors.
    c. A managed investment account.

Our value proposition is unique in that we can give clients access to programs they can't get from our competitors.

Now THAT is leverage (no pun intended).

Apex Outsourcing

In *Apex Outsourcing* (my employee benefits firm I started back in 2003), we completely changed the narrative by showing the client that the true cost of healthcare was not just the premium, but the claims liability plus the premium.

We tapped into our resources and began using a highly sophisticated software program that could calculate the total cost of both the premium and expected claims.

We branded it the *NACH (Net Annual Cost of Healthcare)*.

This algorithm calculated the true projected total cost based on the employee's age, health status, prescription drug usage, network of required doctors, carrier and plan coverage, and delivered a customized package for each individual employee to best suit their needs and their family's needs.

While everyone else was selling off of premium comparisons, we were transparently showing them what the true value of each health plan was, for each employee.

If an employee was on a particular prescription drug, we would search our database to find the health plan that best covered that particular prescription drug.

Then we would cross reference that with our the database of doctors to make sure their primary care physician accepted that particular carrier.

Then we ran a hypothetical claims projection based on each employee's health and calculated what the out-of-pocket costs would be for each employee on an annual basis for each viable plan, then added the annual premium for each plan, and that gave us the *NACH*.

Again, no one was doing this in the small group arena.

DaVinci Financial

With *DaVinci Financial* (my life insurance agency) I developed a proprietary delivery system, offering an *Employee Retirement Program (ERP)* to employees that work for companies with no 401(k) plans.

These are individual accounts set up for employees in which the employer is not faced with restrictions or requirements that a 401(k) plan handcuffs them with, including:

1. No participation requirements.
2. No administration for the employer.
3. No contribution requirements for the employer.
4. No discrimination testing, allowing carveouts.

We essentially took product design that was originally designed for individuals making a minimum of $350,000 per year, and put it on a platform making it available to employees of companies making $35,000 - $65,000 per year.

They can even contribute as little as $100 per month.

We used an indexed universal life insurance policy as the underlying product, and custom engineered its design to produce the maximum allowable cash value accumulation. This design took hours upon hours of hunting-and-pecking to get it dialed in just right. Once we dialed in its design, we created a template so that every policy we used in this program had this cash value maximization feature.

We also built a proprietary software program (which was essentially version 1.0 of what later evolved into *Lionsmark Capital's* algorithm-based software) that can compare the pre-tax equivalent being contributed towards a 401(k) or an IRA, and run backtested models using historical S&P 500 performance, comparing after-tax net outcomes.

No other firm in our space has the platform to effectively offer a program remotely similar to ours, including the delivery system and program installation process.

As I mentioned earlier in this book, in 2019 we were responsible for 38% of *Penn Mutual's* IUL sales in Orange County, California, largely due to this program.

Worsite MGA

In addition, I recently developed a new company – *Worksite MGA* – that offers employees richer benefits at a reduced cost, as well as a substantial savings on FICA taxes and workers' comp premiums for the employer.

This program was originally built for large corporations and municipalities, and I developed a platform to offer it to small businesses.

The core strategy of *Worksite MGA* uses a true *gap plan* that reimburses employees for medical claims that are subject to their major medical plan's deductible.

For example, if the employee previously had a $1,500 deductible, they could downgrade their major medical plan to a new plan with a $5,000 deductible and supplement this deductible liability with a $5,000 *gap plan*, making their deductible liability zero.

The employee would save premium dollars on their major medical plan and use that savings to purchase the *gap plan* through a Section 125 payroll deduction.

In addition, there is a wellness benefit attached to the gap plan, and if the employee is *wellness compliant*, they receive tax-free wellness bonuses from the carrier due to IRC Section 213(d). Often times there is a positive arbitrage created between the wellness bonuses and the after-tax net premium cost of the *gap plan*.

Translation: The employee now has a health insurance plan with $0 deductible exposure and still saves money.

Due to the additional Section 125 plan payroll deductions the *gap plan* creates, the company's gross payroll decreases, saving the employer a substantial amount of money on FICA taxes and workers' compensation insurance because both are calculated off the gross payroll amount.

My firm – *Worksite MGA* – offers this strategy to group health insurance brokers and voluntary benefits reps, giving them a unique offering that their competitors do not have access to.

In fact in many cases, the savings/profit created by the arbitrage between the *gap plan* premium and the Sectiion 213(d) wellness reimbursement can be as much as $50-$300 per month per employee, not to mention the savings they enjoy on the major medical premium.

Voluntary benefits reps can then use that $50-$300 per month savings/profit to fund additional voluntary benefits including life insurance, disability insurance, cancer plans, critical illness plans, etc.

Life insurance agents can use this savings/profit to fund the *Employee Retirement Program (ERP)* I offer through *DaVinci*, and the employer's savings on FICA taxes and workers' comp can be used to fund premium financed life insurance policies on the owners, partners and key employees of the company through *Lionsmark Capital*.

For a 50-employee company, the total savings on FICA taxes and workers' comp is approximately $50,000.

That's $50,000 you can use to fund a $50,000 annual premium life insurance policy.

Or if you were to finance $1,250,000 in cumulative premium at 4.00%, the annual interest would be $50,000 as well. So on a 10-pay life insurance policy, that would be $125,000 in annual premium.

Want to sell $125,000 premium life insurance policies?

Implement this all-inclusive program.

I have branded this all-inclusive program as *The Trifecta Benefit Plan^{TM}*, and I now offer this platform to brokers that were once my competitors, but have now turned into joint venture partners.

Each one of these programs proved to be game changers in the marketplace, and together offer the right solution to the business, the business owner, the employees and the employees' families. In the midst of the COVID-19 pandemic, it was perfectly suited to fulfill everyone's needs, including the brokers and voluntary benefits reps.

The Common Thread

As you can see, the common theme throughout my companies is granting clients access to programs they cannot get elsewhere.

Every one of my value propositions in all my companies is based developing program exclusivity based on a well-developed *USP*.

If you want to build an agency with this level of exclusivity, or at least the perception of exclusivity, you will need to develop a strong *USP*.

You don't need to go crazy like I did and literally create products and software programs. You can simply perfect a unique delivery system, and create the optics of exclusivity.

Here's your homework on how to do it.

Your Homework

I'm sharing examples of what I did with you to give you an idea of what a true *USP* is, so that you can develop your own *USP* and go to market, replicating my format.

So your *homework* on this topic – the topic of creating a unique client experience that is different than your competitors' vanilla sales presentations – is to make a list of everything you think your prospective clients worry about, dislike, distrust and complain about regarding agents that are in your line of work.

Lead off pointing out this *Pink Elephant* in the room.

The format should look like this:

1. Here's how your account is currently set up (establish common ground).

2. Here's the problem with that antiquated process (the *Incumbent Broker Assassination*).

3. Here's how our process is different (your *USP*).

4. Here's why it is superior compared to the outdated way your account is currently set up (*The Benefit*).

5. Here's why we're able to do this and why our competitors don't/can't (*The Inside Story*).

6. Here's an example of one of our clients, and the difference in outcome (*The Testimonial* which creates *Positive Jealousy*).

7. Ask them if they've ever seen anything like this (of course the answer is *no*).

8. Ask them if it makes sense.
9. Ask them if they like the idea.
10. Ask them if they can think of any reason why they wouldn't want to do this.
11. Tell them when you can meet with them next and book the follow up appointment.
12. Require them to sign a commitment letter in order for you to begin working on the proposed solution.
13. Have the guts to walk out if they won't sign.
14. Smile when they beg you to come back, change their mind, and sign… or move on to the next meeting, knowing there are plenty of fish in the sea that will value what you bring to the table.
15. Do not break rules 1-14 under any circumstances.

CHAPTER 7
CONSISTENCY OF CONTENT

One of the things that every sales organization struggles with is the 80/20 rule.

Typically, 20% of your sales force produces 80% of your revenue, and the other 80% of your sales force contributes to you being frustrated 80% of the time in your business life.

Why aren't these agents producing at the level that your top producing agents are, and why are you allowing them to monopolize your time?

It's simple.

They're just not as talented.

Your big hitters usually have several qualities that the rest of your 80% don't have.

They have charisma.

They're great with people.

They tend to evoke feelings of trust and confidence within the prospect due to their people skills and *savoir-faire*.

Now the question is, "What exactly are they doing that the rest of your producers aren't doing?"

Sure, they have these amazing *qualities*, but when you think about a first appointment with a prospect, how long does that appointment typically last?

It's usually about one hour.

One hour is not *that* much time.

So, if your top producers are getting drastically better results than the rest of your crew, the logical question would be, "What exactly are they doing in that first sixty minutes that the rest of your crew isn't doing?"

Is the omission of this extra bonus material the difference between acquiring a client and being kicked to the curb?

What if you could gather the exact content of every single successful sales appointment and distill this content down to the most concise, tight, polished format?

If you could have every single agent replicate that delivery, it would be like cloning your top agents.

This is exactly what I've done.

I did it with a bunch of kids right out of college with no insurance experience, no sales experience, and very limited life experience. Here's why I was able to pull this off.

Every word out of my people's mouths is coached.

The content of our message is always scripted.

Their communication style is a *taught* process.

Their speech inflection and voice tonality is coached and rehearsed.

This is what I call *Consistency of Content*.

Consistency of Content

Every prospect gets the exact same experience during the prospecting process and the sales process, regardless of which one of my agents is interacting with them.

There are several things that make our sales appointments so compelling, but perhaps the most effective component of our sales process has to do with the *style* in which we communicate, even more so than the actual content.

In my businesses, virtually every message we communicate to our prospective clients is planned, rehearsed, and executed with intention and precision.

You know where else you find this level of consistency?

TV infomercials.

You may think TV infomercials are cheesy, however think about how many *Sham-Wow* towels have been purchased through TV infomercials.

Garden Weasels, ProActiv Skin Care products, and *Juiceman* juicers have sold millions of units through this medium.

In 1999, Billy Blanks and his workout DVD program *Tae Bo* did over $75 million in TV infomercial sales, and that was only in his first year.

In 2008, *Bare Minerals* (a TV infomercial cosmetic company) did over $400 million in the fourth quarter. That's over $400 million in sales within a three-month span.

What about *Home Shopping Network*?

A good friend of mine got on Japan's HSN and sold over $200,000 worth of jewelry in twenty minutes.

Why are these numbers so astronomical?

There are several reasons.

The *Sham-Wow* infomercial is the first that comes to mind. It's basically a guy doing a product demo, and he's actually kind of weird looking.

Essentially, here's the format of his message:

1. Here's the problem with most towels.
2. Here's what makes Sham-Wow different.
3. Watch me use it.
4. Watch me use it again.
5. Here are some other ways people have used it.
6. Here's the offer.
7. Buy it now.

Not only is the content concise and straightforward, but the medium of communication through TV infomercials provides the prospect with *Consistency of Content*.

Every viewer experiences the exact same content in the exact same medium with the exact same style of communication every single time.

Now, I am not suggesting that you start running TV infomercials to sell your insurance products.

My point is that the reason this communication medium is so effective is that it's an example of ultimate *Consistency of Content*.

In typical insurance sales where agents are unscripted, there is no *Consistency of Content* whatsoever.

That's why I'm a big believer in using sales video content.

Sales Video Content

Earlier in this book, we talked about the power of video content. Yes, it is extremely powerful in the recruiting proces, but it is even more powerful in the sales process.

That's why I used the example of TV infomercials.

Like them or not, they flat out sell. No doubt about it.

After they communicate the *Benefit*, they'll tell you the *Inside Story* of why the product works so well.

Additionally, they almost always have people telling their story about how the product has helped them, which is the *Testimonial*. In a TV infomercial, they may be paid actors, but it still works.

At the end of the infomercial, they'll create urgency by using a strong call-to-action like, "Call now in the next ten minutes and you'll receive an additional bonus product."

Again, like them or hate them, TV infomercials do a lot of things extremely well from a sales and communication perspective. You can't argue with their sales success, but here's how this concept directly applies to my sales approach.

I've converted the majority of our sales communication with the prospect into short, three-minute videos.

When my agents go out and meet with a prospect face-to-face, they open their laptop and play a series of short videos. Each video communicates a particular concept or strategy to the prospect.

For example, one of our videos illustrates the mechanics of a relatively complex strategy. Here's why this is so effective.

The video is edited to perfection.

It is tight, concise, and very clear.

It is the perfectly-engineered explanation of how the strategy works, so it's much easier for the prospect to understand this relatively complex concept.

That's one of the reasons the product used in this particular strategy has taken such a long time to catch fire in the marketplace.

Almost everyone I've ever heard attempt to explain how the product works does a poor job doing so, including the carrier reps that are supposed to be the primary marketers of the product.

No one could possibly explain the mechanics of this product in less than ten minutes in a live pitch, but I can do it in three minutes in a video. No one could possibly communicate this concept more clearly than a perfectly edited video either.

The other great thing about using video communication in the sales process is that videos are always consistent in both their content and delivery.

They are 100% perfect, 100% of the time.

Using sales video content is the ultimate way to ensure *C.O.C.* within a sales organization.

Videos Provide Ultimate Consistency of Content

One of the challenges in professional sales is that you're relying on human beings to communicate concepts, and human beings are inconsistent.

Unless they are incredibly disciplined and scripted, they're going to have a slightly different sales approach each time they step into a sales appointment, which means they have no *Consistency of Content*.

Not only do they lack *Consistency of Content*, but they also lack *Consistency of Delivery*.

Have you ever noticed that some days you're *in the zone*? Have you also noticed that some days, you're just *off*?

As human beings, we all have *off* days from time to time because we're susceptible to our emotions.

If you get into an argument with your spouse on the way out the door that morning, you're probably going to have an *off* day.

If you just lost a loved one, you're probably going to have an *off* day that day too.

Same thing if you're feeling a little under the weather.

Human beings have *off days*, but videos never have *off days*.

Videos deliver the same perfect message every single time, and they never babble and get off track, lose their confidence, or forget what to say. Once edited, they are perfect.

Videos Reduce Training Time

The other thing about video communication in the sales process is that it allows you to build an army of new agents that are game-ready almost instantaneously.

It doesn't matter if it's me pushing play or a brand new agent pushing play. Sure, I'm more talented, more knowledgeable, and more confident than a brand-new agent, but it doesn't matter if the first appointment is structured so that the videos do the majority of the content articulation.

Videos Develop a Better Relationship Dynamic

As I just said, the video is the one delivering the sales pitch, not the agent. In my sales process, after each three-minute video is played, my agents chat with the prospect about the content they just viewed *together*.

This chatty conversation is much less combative than when an agent is trying to *close* the prospect in a typical sales scenario.

When the prospect watches a video *with* the agent sitting side-by-side (as opposed to sitting across the conference room table in opposition), the prospect feels like the agent is on *their side*.

The prospect wants to talk about the content they just saw in the video *with* the agent, versus in a typical sales appointment, the agent attempts to talk the prospect into the deal.

The harder the agent tries to convince the prospect, the more desperate the agent appears.

In the dating world, there is nothing more repulsive to a woman than a desperate man, and in the sales world, there is nothing more repulsive to a prospect than a desperate sales rep.

Videos have the power to completely change the dynamic of the conversation and the relationship between the two parties.

There are several other subconscious triggers that videos pull in the sales process.

Let's discuss a few.

Human Beings Are Obsessed with Video Monitors

I don't know why this is, but it is an undisputed fact that people are obsessed with looking at video monitors.

If there is a TV screen, regardless of what's playing on it, people are compelled to look at it. They can't help themselves.

As I mentioned earlier in this book, when you're on an airplane and the flight attendant does the seat belt demonstration right before take-off, nobody pays attention. But when that exact same demonstration is playing on a video screen, more than half of the people stare at the monitor, watching the video.

These are the same people that would totally ignore the flight attendant standing in the aisle doing a live demo.

A friend of mine once told me that he was at church one Sunday morning – he goes to one of those mega-churches you see on TV with tens of thousands of attendees in the audience – there were two big projection screens on stage with a live video feed of the pastor playing on them.

Well, apparently the pastor was delivering his message and he started poking fun at the people sitting in the front row because though he was standing right in front of them, they all looked right past him, watching him on the huge projection screen on the stage.

The pastor jokingly said to them, "Hello! Guys, I'm right here in front of you. Why are you looking at the video feed of me on the screen when I'm right here?"

This story illustrates my point about our obsession with video monitors and video screens.

We just can't stop looking at them.

That's why sales videos are so powerful.

As illogical as it sounds, we've found that our prospects are more engaged with the content in the video (played on a laptop computer) than they are when a live human being delivers the exact same content.

I know this is somewhat counterintuitive because you would think there would be a stronger connection with a live person delivering content, versus a video screen.

Ironically, it's just the opposite.

My Initial Concern with Using Videos

Initially, when I started testing this process, my concern was that business owners might view this process as being cold and impersonal.

I feared that they would get bored sitting through so many videos. The reaction we got from our prospects was just the opposite. They absolutely loved it.

If you're running an agency, using video sales content enables you to not only increase your agents' closing percentage in the field, but it also allows you to train new agents and get them game-ready much faster because it allows you to control what and how your message is being communicated to prospects without you even being there.

It also gives you the ability to clone top producers because the video content is what is closing the business, not the personalities of your agents.

You Can Produce Your Own Videos

Let's discuss how you can construct your own sales videos.

I'm not going to say it's easy.

It is not, but here's my process.

I start by whipping out a yellow pad, mapping out what I want to communicate, drawing stick figures, boxes and arrows.

This process allows me to *see* what I want the client to see.

Next up is developing the best chronological order in which I want to unveil my message, which starts with understanding what the client already believes in and accepts.

The goal is to tie the *familiar* to my new *unfamiliar concept*.

Here's the framework of my communication process:

1. Establish agreement on an existing concept they already believe in.
2. Explain why this existing concept makes so much sense.
3. Show them how the new concept shares parallel beliefs with the existing concept they already believe in.
4. Confirm that they already believe in the existing concept, therefore they must also believe in the new parallel concept.
5. Confirm that they lose nothing by implementing this new concept, that there is no risk, and that there are only benefits.
6. Confirm that the incumbent cannot offer them this.
7. Confirm that they have run out of reasons to not do this.

This process is something I've developed over the last ten years, and it is called *Checkmate*.

Checkmate is a chronological series of questions I ask a prospect that results in only one outcome: To do business with me, only me, and no one else.

I was initially reticent to use the term *Checkmate* for fear that it implies an *I Win, You Lose* intention.

To clarify, the only intention I have is to create a mutually beneficial *Win-Win* for both me and my client.

The reason I love the term *Checkmate* is that it so clearly articulates the final outcome. There is literally no other option but to buy from me.

For example, in one of my companies, we sell voluntary benefits. These are products that the employer offers to their employees, and the employee pay for 100%.

They cost the business owner nothing.

Some of these products cover medical expenses from an employee benefits standpoint, and some of them are life insurance-based products used to create a tax-free retirement income

With some of these products, if the employees purchase them via payroll deduction, the business actually saves money on FICA taxes because the premiums are paid for pre-tax, so the company's gross payroll is reduced.

FICA taxes (7.65% at the time this book was written) are calculated based on the total gross payroll. Workers' comp premiums are also calculated based on the total gross payroll.

Hence, when the total gross payroll is reduced by the payroll deductions that come from the employees purchasing voluntary benefits, the business saves a substantial amount of money on FICA taxes and workers' comp premiums.

Statistically, half of the employees will buy, so all we need to do is get the employer to grant us access to their employees, and ultimately, employer will ultimately save money on both FICA taxes and workers' comp.

Despite this no-lose proposition, it's not as easy as it sounds. Ask any *Aflac* rep and they'll confirm this statement.

The concept of *voluntary benefits* is often times new to the employer, so we have to link the unfamiliar to the familiar.

Here's how I designed our *Checkmate* sales process:

Me: Do you offer health insurance to your employees?

Them: Of course.

Me: What about to their dependents, who pays for that?

Them: They do.

Me: So as long as they pay for it, you don't have a problem offering it?

Them: Yeah, basically.

Me: Okay. Do you have employees with families, or is everyone single?

Them: Most of our employee have families.

Me: Do they rely on one income to support the family, or two?

Them: Two.

Me: Are they rich, or are they living paycheck to paycheck?

Them: Paycheck to paycheck.

Me: So if one of them dies, can the family live off one paycheck when They were barely getting by on two?

Them: No, they would be financially destroyed.

Me: Do you think most of your employees have enough life insurance?

Them: Probably not.

Me: Would you have any problem with offering life insurance to your employees, in the exact same way you offer dependent health insurance?

Them: No, I have no problem with that.

Checkmate!

You just sold the group a voluntary benefits package.

No hard selling.

No pressure.

Just a series of simple questions.

Now, if you were going to produce a sales video to communicate this message, this is the recipe for the format.

Agreement #1:
You already offer dependent health insurance coverage, as long as the employees pay for it.

Agreement #2:
Your employees need two incomes, and if an employee died, the family could not survive off just one income.

Parallel Concept:
Offering your employees health insurance coverage for their dependents, as long as they pay for it, is categorically a *Voluntary Benefit*.

Realization:
You're already offering a voluntary benefit.

Parallel Assumption:
Offering voluntary life insurance is the same as offering employee-paid dependent health insurance coverage.

New Agreement:
You should offer a suite of voluntary benefits, not just dependent health insurance and life insurance.

CHAPTER 8

GO F*** YOURSELF

Now before you go all crazy on me, understand that my version of the F-word – F*** – is an acronym for *Forget Your Misconceptions About* something you think you understand.

Forget Your Misconceptions About challenges.

Forget Your Misconceptions About goals.

Forget Your Misconceptions About your *why*.

Forget Your Misconceptions About yourself.

We all need to recondition and rewire our brains from all the negative nonsense we hear every day, and change the way we perceive things, including the way we perceive ourselves.

F*** Challenges

Forget Your Misconceptions About challenges.

A winning-oriented perspective is very different than a losing-oriented perspective. When the COVID-19 pandemic struck and people all over the world were quarantined at home, I heard all kinds of whining.

People would say, "I'm so bored."

"No one will take my call," agents would say.

While everyone was sitting around sulking, I decided to use the *downtime* to develop a brand new market with a brand new approach.

I was already used to running virtual sales meetings over the phone and via screenshare, so that was nothing new.

But when the longest bull market in U.S. history crashed on March 12, 2020 and the stock market experienced the steepest one-day fall since the crash in 1987, I knew I needed to accelerate my recalibration process.

A week later, the market closed with the price of oil at -$35 a barrel. This was the first time in history that U.S. oil futures fell into negative territory. On April 20, 2020 the price for *West Texas Intermediate (WTI)* crude fell to -$37.63 a barrel. Just a few months earlier in January, it sold for $61.22 a barrel.

During the COVID-19 crash, I wasn't *bored* at all, and I sure as hell didn't sit around sulking. I was looking for opportunities.

In fact, I was working even harder during the quarantine lockdown that I was pre-Coronavirus pandemic.

I also looked for opportunities that didn't exist before.

I was on the phone with my business partner everyday discussing an untapped market we had planned to venture into over the next year or so, but the COVID-19 crash greatly accelerated our timeline.

In many ways, it forced us to more intensely focus on what we needed to shift our focus to anyway, and this reallocation of our time pushed us to launch yet another company together.

Sometimes challenges force you to do what you knew you needed to do in the first place, and they accelerate your timeline, which is why I embrace challenges now.

Bull markets often breed complacency and diminish urgency, whereas *bear markets* breed the kind of urgency that turns *champions* into *legends*.

When I was a kid, I loved playing soccer in the rain because I knew my opponents would be whining and complaining about how slippery it was and how much harder it was to play well.

It was obviously just as slippery for me too, but because I knew the other team felt they were at a *disadvantage*, I felt that gave me an *advantage* over them. It was a mind game.

It's the same thing in business.

Great fortunes are often made during great tumultuous times, because this is when the strong shine the brightest.

It's also when most people bury their heads in the sand.

So F*** challenges.

Forget your misconceptions about all of these so-called challenges, because they are actually opportunities for you to pull ahead of everyone else.

Let's talk about your misconceptions about goals.

F* Goals**

Nothing happens due to *goals*.

If you have a goal to make a million dollars – whether that's per year, per month or per week – congratulations on your ambition, but it's all meaningless.

Forget Your Misconceptions About your so-called *goals*.

Most goal setting programs are just pie-in-the-sky dreams.

In theory, there's nothing wrong with setting goals.

I certainly set goals, but my process is very different than what most people think of regarding goal setting.

Every goal I've every successfully achieved was merely a side effect of three things coming together at the same time:

1. Doing the right things.
2. Doing them at the right time.
3. Doing them with the right people.

You can do the right things at the wrong time, and you'll fail.

You can do the right things with the wrong people, and you'll most likely fail as well.

Some people think creating a dream board – pasting pictures of expensive crap they want to buy on a piece of cardboard – is going to make their dreams come true.

It's nonsense. Same thing with your *why*.

F* Your Why**

I always cracks me up when I hear these neo-hippies in business say, "It's all about my *why*."

That kind of esoteric nonsense holds zero value.

Just because you watched a 30-minute Simon Sinek *TED Talk* doesn't make you a marketing expert or a motivational guru.

Is your *why* important?

Yes, but not in the way most people think.

If you are building an army and developing a culture, then sharing your greater purpose with your team so they can rally behind a cause can be powerful. Communicating and reinforcing your mission to all the players on your team can literally create a *movement*.

But when it comes to prospective clients, they only care whether or not you are the best in your field, not whether your *spirit animal* aligns with theirs.

To illustrate what I mean by this, imagine if your child was abducted by a terrorist.

The terrorist tells the hostage negotiator, "I need $1 million. Every hour that goes by where I don't have the money, the kid loses a finger. If I don't have the money by 5:00 P.M., I cut his head off with a steak knife."

If this was your child, would you care about the hostage negotiator's *why*?

Hell no.

All you'd care about is whether or not they can get your child back home to you safely. You would only care about the hostage negotiator's ability to perform, not their intentions and life purpose.

In addition, you would only have faith in them if you were convinced they were the *best-of-the-best* in their field.

I apologize for the overly graphic example, but the reason I chose to use an uber-extreme scenario is to get you to see the irrelevance of a person's *why* in the midst of a high-stakes crisis.

The only time anyone cares about your *why* is after you've proven that can deliver a better outcome than your competition.

And even then, your *why* is a novelty at best. It's not a decision-driver.

For example, *Toms* shoe company made a big splash with their *Get One, Give One* campaign wherein they donate a pair of shoes to a needy child for every pair of shoes a consumer purchases. This type of *Socially Responsible Business (SRB)* does create a buzz, and is an admirable thing. But I can guarantee you that if *Toms* shoes were ugly, no one would buy them despite their *socialpreneurship* business model.

The product or service has to be desirable enough to stand on its own merits, despite any heartwarming why.

Now, once you establish yourself as the only one your clients (notice I said *clients*, not *prospects*) should be doing business with, sharing with them your greater mission and your calling can be an extremely powerful way to solidify them as a client, but it will not win them over as a client initially.

So F*** your *why* in the context of thinking it your life story will influence someone to buy. There is literally no value there.

You need to focus on the prospect's *why* instead of gushing about your own *why*. Identify how their life will improve by doing business with you, and masterfully articulate *why* it will improve.

The only *why's* you should be thinking about in regards to communicating with a prospect are:

1. Why you understand their current situation.
2. Why their current plan is not good enough.
3. Why and how they will suffer if they don't switch out.
4. Why they need to switch to you, only you, and no one else.

Once you have communicated this with full confidence, authenticity and articulated the *Benefit, Inside Story* and *Testimonial*, communicating your why can create a very powerful solidifying bond between you and the client.

For example, after I have established myself as the only one they should be doing business with, I will share with them why I got into the financial services field as a profession.

131

Two years after I put out the *First Edition* of this book, I had a rude awakening.

I hired a so-called financial advisor once my first insurance agency had taken off and things were going well. He implemented a strategy that was supposed to save me a ton of money in taxes and involved me purchasing seventeen life insurance policies – sixteen of them on my employees and 1099 agents, and a $20 million one on myself.

The strategy was supposed to give me some massive corporate tax deductions and also grow a tax-free corporate portfolio housed inside these seventeen corporate-owned life insurance policies.

I was contributing over $200,000 per year into this strategy, and I did it without truly understanding how the program worked. I just trusted the advisor.

Three years into this program, I decided to hire a tax attorney to come in and do an internal audit and explain to me how all the moving parts worked.

After a week of audit, the attorney came to me and said, "Darren, I have bad news for you. You've contributed over $600,000 into this program, your account value is zero, and the program is completely structured improperly. You have to unwind the entire thing, and on top of that, you now owe the IRS and the State of California $330,000 in back-taxes, penalties and interest."

This financial advisor lost me $930,000 in three years.

I was so pissed and embarrassed, but I decided to turn lemons into lemonade and I became vigilant about learning everything I could about every type of life insurance policy including how the policy expenses were charged, the different product chassis options, the different crediting methods, and where all the bodies were buried. I became obsessed with learning everything about everything as it pertained to how a life insurance policy was structured.

Then I wrote a book about it called *Ouch – How My Financial Advisor Lost Me $930,000 In Three Years*. That book was the genesis of my launching *DaVinci Financial*.

I know how confusing investments, retirement planning and life insurance policies are, and I know how it feels to get screwed by a financial advisor.

That's why I'm so passionate about the work we do at *DaVinci*. That's why I'm so passionate about the work that Jeff and I do at *Lionsmark Capital*.

My entire mission is to teach our clients how the world of investments, retirement planning and life insurance actually works because I know first-hand how it feels to be in their position – the feeling of being rich in income, but helpless in regards to understanding how a portfolio actually works.

That's my *why*.

Powerful, but only powerful if I can prove that my strategies are superior and proprietary, and only if I can prove that I can deliver my clients a better outcome than my competition.

Again, use your why as a client solidifier, not an initial marketing tool.

F*** Yourself

You must *Forget Your Misconceptions About* who you are and develop a new understanding of who you are, which starts with achieving clarity regarding who you want to be.

There is one thing every uber-successful person has: Clarity.

They have clarity regarding who they are, what they stand for, and where they're going.

This alone will not make you successful, but without this, it is damn near impossible for you to become successful, and it starts with understanding the root of your insecurities.

Your insecurities are largely rooted in three events from your childhood:

1. How your classmates reacted when you made a mistake.
2. How your parents reacted when you made a mistake.
3. The first time someone broke your heart.

If your classmates made fun of you publicly when you made an embarrassing mistake, you probably went in one of several directions:

1. You projected your anger onto others and became a bully.

2. You became withdrawn, afraid to take risks and make mistakes.

3. You became the class clown to draw attention away from your blunders, getting people to focus on your antics instead of your mistakes.

4. You became a perfectionist so no one could ever make fun of you again.

If your parents expressed extreme anger or disappointment when you made a mistake, or if they made you feel like their love and acceptance was contingent on your performance, you either became:

1. A people-pleaser who constantly tries to make others like you due to your low self-esteem.

2. A couch potato, feeling like you could never please anyone, so you stopped trying altogether.

3. Hyper-driven and success-obsessed driven by the fear of not being accepted unless you are the best.

4. A stage parent, putting immense pressure on your own kids, vicariously living through their successes, because that's what you feel your parents did to you.

The first time you got your heart broken influenced your entire approach to romantic relationships, even as an adult. You either became:

1. Withdrawn and shy, afraid to love again.

2. Cold and unwilling to let anyone get close to you for fear that they would one day leave you.

3. A tease or a player, finding pleasure in getting others to chase you, then dumping them before they dump you.

4. More sensitive and compassionate towards other people's feelings because you don't want others to experience the heartbreak that you experienced.

As you reconnect with these childhood experiences, though they seem meaningless to you today, they are the root of why you have confidence in some areas, and massive insecurities in others.

It is imperative to understand these roots, because once you understand them as an adult, you can reorganize and recategorize these experiences on your emotional hard drive, and finally let go of your negative emotional connections from your past.

You see, confidence is not *created*.

Confidence is *realized*.

Once you *realize* that most of the things you're insecure about are meaningless, you can liberate yourself from your negative past and develop a strong resolve in who you are.

So what does all of this have to do with building a successful insurance agency?

Not only do you need confidence to be successful with clients, but you also need confidence to lead an army. This is done by coming to grips with your negative past and ending the negative emotional cycle brought upon you by your insecurities. You need to realize true confidence.

I'm not talking about *fabricated bravado* or *fake it till you make it* posturing either.

I'm talking about *true confidence* – the kind of confidence that comes from knowing who you are and what you stand for – which can be summed up in one word: Authenticity.

F*** Confidence

Forget Your Misperceptions About confidence.

Fake confidence is loud, obnoxious and braggadocious.

True confidence is actually calm, quiet and *authentic*.

It *looks* authentic because only true confidence *is* authentic.

Truly confident people go *all-in* because they have an unwavering belief in who they are and what they are doing, and they don't have to yell the obvious from the mountain tops.

They're not yearning for approval or acceptance, so they don't allow themselves to be influenced by the other people's novice ideas about how something *should* be done.

They are secure in their own methods.

They don't *mirror* the client. *They* are the ones that dictate the pace and tone of the interaction, not the other way around.

A confident person sets the emotional state of the environment, they don't *succumb* to the prospect's emotional state and mirror their energy.

They are not led. They lead.

Confident people are also extremely transparent and openly talk about their past failures and past insecurities. They also respectfully share their perspectives on things even when they know their opinion is different than the *public opinion*.

They are comfortable to do so because they are not influenced by the masses. *They* are the ones who are the influencers.

Confidence In Leadership

A confident leader is willing to admit when they are wrong, and take responsibility for the team's outcome, especially when the outcome is poor.

A confident leader is also willing to kill his existing model if they learn that a better one exists, and a better one always exists. Often times people's egos get in the way of innovation because they think they know it all.

Their past success gives them the illusion that they've *arrived*.

But a real leader knows that constant innovation is necessary to stay ahead of the curve. By definition, you never really ever *arrive* because the landscape is constantly changing.

You will always have some agents that get upset with this dynamic environment because generally speaking, people resist change. It either scares them, or they don't like it because it requires more work.

It is certainly easier to just stay the course and continue to operate within your comfort zone.

But here's what many people don't get.

You must destroy what is *good* to create what is *great*.

Then you have to destroy what is *great* to create what is *indisputably the best*.

Then you have to destroy what is *indisputably the best* to create something that is *proprietary* – one of a kind.

Once you have something that is *proprietary* and *indisputably the best*, you have to continually evolve and improve it in order to stay ahead of the curve, because the world is never static. This means relative to an everchanging landscape, you're either getting *better* or you're getting *worse*. There is no such thing as staying the *same*.

Even if you're already #1, you must continually create new products, programs and models that don't exist.

That's how you stay #1.

The old saying, "*If it ain't broke, don't fix it,*" is what taxi cab companies said before *Uber* came along.

This commitment to constantly improve an already-great system is exhausting, and in that moment, it seems unnecessary.

It creates mental and physical exhaustion for the innovator, beyond what non-innovators can possibly imagine. But this is where champions are made.

I always say that *convenience* is a poor environment to create *greatness* in because a convenient environment doesn't push you to innovate.

It takes great discipline to make seemingly unnecessary changes to stay ahead of the curve, but innovators and *Thought Leaders* need to constantly prove to themselves that they place more value on *their vision* than they do on what *other people* think.

One of my favorite Latin sayings is *Non Ducor Duca*, which translated to English means *I Am Not Led. I Lead.*

But how you lead your team is *secondary*.

The *primary* focus needs to be on how you lead yourself.

I'm now going to share with you some exercises I do to keep my growth game strong and my mind right.

Five Questions I Ask Myself Each Month

I start off each month asking myself a series of five questions, because my answers to these questions is what keeps me on track.

<u>Question #1: What is repeatedly happening that makes me want to punch someone in the face?</u>

Don't laugh. I'm dead serious.

It's important to identify what areas of your business are making you miserable, angry, resentful and preventing you from being in the right head space.

If your mind is cluttered with frustration about non-essential things, you cannot innovate and thrive.

Right now, are you spending a disproportionate amount of time and energy obsessing about a person or a process that is not moving your business in the right direction?

If it's a process, you need to change the process.

If it's a person, you need to either get rid of the person, or change your rules of engagement with that person.

If you do nothing and accept that bad behavior and/or the inefficiencies of your process, things will not get better. They will get worse.

You must cut out the cancer quickly.

<u>Question #2: What irrelevant things am I wasting my time on?</u>

First of all, you have to define what *irrelevant* is.

An easy way to make this distinction is to ask yourself, "Will this even matter three years from now?"

If the answer is *no*, that's probably a good indicator that you shouldn't be wasting your time obsessing about it.

I have a saying that reminds me of how important making this distinction is: To do something is to not do something else.

There are many things you may be spending your time doing right now that aren't necessarily *bad* things to do, but if you reprioritized your To-Do-List, you would find that your time spent on something else would give you a greater return on investment.

Just as you may have a *To-Do List*, you must also have a *Do-Not-Do List*. If I have ten things that I want to get done, but I only have time to do three of them, that means I need to put seven things on my Do-Not-Do-List.

It doesn't mean there's anything wrong with doing those things, but they are not in the top three. If you do one of the seven on your Do-Not-Do-List, by definition, it means that you failed to do one of the three most important things that you should be doing.

It is much easier to clarify what these things are if you have a list of *rules*, which I will share with you in a moment.

Let the rules dictate whether or not you are misappropriating your time and effort, and if you aren't going to care about something three years from now, there's a good chance it's *irrelevant* in the bigger picture.

If it is, put it on your *Do-Not-Do-List*.

Question #3: What have I recently eliminated from my life that needed to be eliminated?

There is a tremendous value in realizing that the elimination of all things unnecessary improves your business and quality of life.

If you have been proactive about effective elimination, taking time to remind yourself that you made the right decision will give you increased clarity and empower you to do more of it.

Revisiting ballsy decisions you've made in the past, especially in the area of ridding yourself of non-essential activities and energy-sucking people, gives you confirmation you made the right decision.

No one has ever said, "I wish I would have kept that jackass on my team."

Question #4: What has happened in my business that seemed like a setback at first, but turned out to be a blessing?

It is easy for us to fall into the habit of focusing on everything that didn't pan out the way we had hoped.

I believe that sometimes God doesn't give you what you wanted because He thought you deserved better.

Many times in both my business life and my personal life, things didn't pan out with people the way I wanted them to.

But in retrospect, maybe God heard conversations that I didn't, and removed certain people from my life to protect me from future harm.

I have experienced this so many times.

You have to kiss a lot of frogs.

If my last business partner didn't remove himself, I wouldn't have my current business partner, Jeff.

If my first wife didn't remove herself, I wouldn't have my current wife, Emilia.

Sometimes you are blessed with a massive upgrade without you even doing the replacing.

Any betrayal, departure, rejection you may have experienced with people has created a void – an empty seat – to be filled by someone greater.

If you're in the middle of going through this right now, I know it's hard to believe this is the case. Heartbreak is a terrible ordeal to go through, so if you're hurting right now, I know it sucks.

When a person you were so close to at one point leaves you, it is difficult to see the forest through the trees in that moment.

But you know why divorce and business partnership dissolutions are so expensive?

It's because they're worth it.

Question #5: Is there a new opportunity I should explore?

The world is constantly evolving.

So must an entrepreneur's business model.

In the insurance industry, things are constantly changing. Tax laws, regulatory restrictions, underwriting allowances, carrier products – the list goes on and on.

Sometimes these changes create a void in the marketplace that no else is prepared for. Being first-in can create a big opportunity for those that can identify the void and be the first to fill it.

Be open to these new opportunities.

Now, sometimes you will go through periods where there the timing is not right, and forcing a new opportunity just for the sake of exploring a new opportunity is not wise. Don't be so intent on looking for *red* that you see *maroon* and call it *red* just because you feel you have to meet a self-imposed *new opportunity quota*.

You have to be patient and selective.

For a baseball player, there are times to look for certain pitches, and times to lay off certain pitches.

I was a power hitter while playing baseball at Loyola Marymount University, meaning my role was to drive in RBIs. If I found myself in a 2-and-0 count (two balls and zero strikes), I could be very selective.

I only looked for one pitch: Fastball, up and in.

I opened my stance ever so slightly in a 2-and-0 count, and if that pitcher threw me my pitch, I was geared up to jack that thing out of the park. But if he threw me some off-speed, down and out crap, I would lay off that pitch, even if it was a strike.

That wasn't *my* pitch.

With a 2-and-0 count, I could be selective.

There's nothing worse for a clean-up hitter to do than chase the wrong pitch with a 2-and-0 count. Same thing in business.

But if you get that fastball up-and-in on a 2-and-0 count, you'd better be geared up for it, and you'd better go *big fly*.

No *check swings* on a 2-and-0 count.

In business, if you happen to find the right void, at the right time, and you're partnered with the right people, you can hit a grand slam, but your *opportunity radar* must be turned on 24/7.

My Leadership Principles

I promised you that I would share some of the key principles I live by – both in my business life, as well as my personal life – when it comes to making my *To-Do List* and my *Do-Not-Do List*, so here are a few.

1. The best way to sabotage your success is to *play* before you *work*.
2. The best way to lose *big dollar* opportunities is to haggle over the *pennies*.
3. The best way to lose the *war* is to fight the *wrong battles*.
4. The best way to win the war is to win it *before it even starts*.
5. The best way to ruin your reputation is to *take* before you *give*.
6. The best way to strike a better deal is to *over-deliver* before you *negotiate*.
7. The best way to receive a *favor* is to never ask for one.
8. The best way to receive a *compliment* is to be the first to give one.

9. The best way to be the recipient of generosity is to be the *most generous person* in the room, with *no expectation of reciprocation.*

10. The best way to receive *massive blessings* is to feel *entitled to none of them.*

Speaking of entitlement, in the next chapter I will talk about the challenges of running an agency of 1099 agents.

As you have probably already experienced, 1099 agents often feel entitled to everything and expect you to provide them with training, administrative support, sales support, free leads, psychological counseling, a shoulder to cry on, and larger commission splits that come out of your pocket.

They often violate each of these ten rules have I listed above, and if you expect them not to, you will be setting yourself up for disappointment.

At times, you will question whether or not it's even worth having 1099 agents.

The key is set boundaries and a set of rules of engagement that work for you, and also work for them.

Welcome to *Chapter 9: 1099 Independent Contractors.*

CHAPTER 9

1099 INDEPENDENT CONTRACTORS

You can't make a 1099 do anything.

Have you ever heard an insurance agency owner say this?

Have you ever said this yourself?

Let me tell you the real deal here.

It's true.

You can't force a 1099 independent contractor to do anything.

Well, you can try, but you'll most likely get sued for violating *Department Of Labor* law. The *DOL* has a list of questions that establish the employer-employee relationship, disqualifying the *independent contractor* categorization.

The insurance industry has kinda-sorta gotten a hall pass on this issue, but to the letter of the law, the majority of insurance agencies are in violation of the independent contractor smell test.

For example, you cannot control what the agent does or how the job is done. They will measure the type of instruction given, the degree of the instruction, any evaluation systems, and – you guessed it – training.

Add a litigious, disgruntled ex-agent into this equation, and you are almost guaranteed to get sued at some point, unless you have everything spelled out in your 1099 agreement, and even then, anyone can sue anyone for any reason.

So for all you *Bobby Knight* type leaders, your days are numbered. Sadly, even if you take more of a *John Wooden* approach, the fact that you're teaching your players how to tie their shoes could be considered too much control and instruction.

It's a damn shame the world has come to this, but this is the world we live in today. So if you can't force your agents to be successful, how are you going to build and run a successful agency?

It's not easy.

In the beginning, when I first started developing my agency, it was a major challenge. I remember the first sales crew I had.

On the first day our office was officially opened, I reviewed the phone script with the team, identified the lists to call from, and pulled the trigger on the starting gun.

Guess what happened.

No one picked up the phone to dial.

No one did anything.

There I was, sitting in the middle of my sales floor with six agents, waiting for them to do something. They just sat there, fumbling their papers.

One of them even whipped out a magazine and started reading it instead of making calls.

I was so pissed.

Believe me, I wanted to go *Bobby Knight* on their ass.

I didn't, but I sure as hell wanted to.

Have you ever been in this situation?

It's frustrating, isn't it?

One thing I've learned about effective leadership is that you cannot expect your people to do something that you're not modeling yourself.

True leadership is about jumping into the trenches with your people and dialing alongside them. Leaders that don't lead by example are not true leaders.

There are five key rules when it comes to inspiring independent contractors that I'll discuss right now.

Rule #1: Lead By Example

A true leader sets the tone.

A true leader says, "Watch me do it, and do the same."

A true leader says, "Here, I'll do it with you."

Your people – especially the independent contractors – will respect you more when they see that you're practicing what you're preaching.

They will become inspired to do the same.

You can't *manage* an independent contractor, but you can *inspire* an independent contractor. The only way people get inspired is when they see someone else accomplishing something that they want to accomplish, too.

That's where *Leading By Example* comes in.

Your people are secretly asking themselves two simple things:

1. Can I do this?
2. Is it worth doing?

The first question cannot be answered with words.

It must be proven with action, by showing them a live example. They must say to themselves, "I saw them do it, and if they can do it, then so can I."

The next step is you need to watch them do it, coaching them along the way. They'll wrap up the day saying, "I did it with my leader, and surprisingly, it wasn't that hard. I can do this!"

The second question is a question that rarely gets answered, and it's the reason why so many people quit the insurance business.

Are you illustrating to your brand-new agents exactly what they get if they follow your system to the tee?

If not, they're going to quit because question number two never got answered.

What exactly are they going to get after one year of doing this grunt work?

What about two years, five years, and ten years?

When we bring on a brand-new agent, we walk them through an *Electronic Truth Teller*. This is a formula-driven spreadsheet that automatically calculates their commission potential based on four variables:

1. Number of dials per hour.
2. Number of dials per week.
3. Booking percentage on the phone.
4. Closing percentage in the field.

I base this calculation assuming several constants, such as:

1. Average group size.
2. Average premium per employee.
3. Average employee participation.

These calculations project the agent's hypothetical commission amounts and extrapolates it out over years one, two, three, four, five, and ten years.

Agents need to see real, hard numbers every step along the way, assuming they're doing the volume of activity they committed to doing. The agent is the one that decides on their variables, including volume of activity and skill level acquired.

If you build a commission calculator, I highly suggest you have a disclaimer on the calculator/spreadsheet that says something to the effect of:

> *This spreadsheet is not a recommended schedule for anyone to follow. It is not enforced upon any agent. All agents are 1099 independent contractors and are neither managed by any company, supervisor, or manager. Independent agents do not report to anyone and are not accountable to any schedule of any kind. All cells in this Excel spreadsheet are adjustable at each user's discretion. This document is intended for an independent agent to model hypothetical commission projections for their own independent benefit and self-evaluation, not for any other purposes.*

It's sad that you have to be this stringent in regards to the 1099 issue, but you do. Every document you publish must have this type of appropriate disclaimer on it.

Okay, back to *Leading By Example*.

You must show them that they can do it. Just model the activity for them first, and follow it up by coaching them through the process while they do the exact same thing you just did.

One time, I actually walked onto my sales floor and announced to my producers that I was going to make cold-calls with them for thirty minutes.

You should have seen the looks on their faces, especially the new guys who have only been with my firm for a couple of weeks. I'm the president of the firm, but I hopped right in there with my crew.

As the president of my agency, I had gained my people's respect because they knew I'm wasn't above grinding it out in the trenches with them.

They still couldn't believe that I would cold-call with them.

I even announced that anyone that made more calls than I made in that thirty-minute period would get to go to lunch with me on Friday, my treat.

You should have seen these agents blazing the phones.

I personally made thirty-one dials in that thirty minutes, but six of the agents actually beat me. These are the same agents that average thirty dials per hour, and they did more than that in just 30-minutes.

Why?

Because they got excited to see their leader jump in and do it with them. In addition, you must show them exactly what they're going to get (commission-wise) if they diligently and consistently repeat this activity.

This is where the *Electronic Truth Teller* comes into play.

You can't just give them hypothetical approximations. Your calculations must be statistically based, not pie-in-the-sky hypotheticals.

So, without rule number one, you will fail miserably at inspiring independent contractors. You'll live the majority of your business life frustrated and resentful, and it will be entirely your own fault.

But if you follow rule one to the tee, you'll build a super agency and become the hero to your people.

Rule #2: Treat Them Like Partners, Not Employees

One of the biggest mistakes I see agency owners make is that they treat their 1099 agents like employees.

They're not your employees.

If you treat them as such, it's like trying to herd cats.

It's impossible.

Plus, they'll resent you for it because they (just like you) became an independent contractor because they didn't want to have to answer to a boss.

You're not their boss, and if you want to argue that point, you'd better hope the *Department Of Labor* doesn't find out, or you'll be paying fines and penalties in the tens of thousands of dollars.

What you are is a *resource* for your agents.

You've got to treat them like business partners.

In a business where you both have skin in the game, which is what you have in a 1099-driven insurance agency, you are essentially partners in the deal – not *equity partners*, but partners nonetheless.

You've got to create an environment where it's easy for them to succeed because when they succeed, you succeed.

The easier you make it for them to be successful, the more revenue they'll create, which ultimately is how you make a living as an agency owner.

I know a lot of people are surprised to hear me say things like this because I have a reputation for being a hard-ass.

I'm not a hard-ass in the sense of being the boss.

What I really am is a clarifier.

My job is to clarify to my producers what the end result will be based on the actions they're taking.

In fact, in my quarterly planning sessions with them, I have them set their own goals.

I don't have sales quotas in my agency.

I let each agent tell me what their goals are, and I help them formulate an action plan around the goals that they set.

As great a motivator as I've been told that I am, the reality is that I've never been able to successfully guilt or convince someone into producing more, at least not long-term.

So, rule two is all about how you make your producers *feel*.

Does that sound *touchy-feely* or what?

I know, I know, but like it or not, even the self-proclaimed tough agents are emotionally needy and *touchy-feely*.

You need to be smart about how you treat your people. You'd be surprised how big of a role emotions play in people's everyday decision-making process.

The moment they feel that you're not on their side, they'll turn against you, and the more time that elapses where they feel like this, the more they will distance themselves from you.

Ultimately, they will quit, and it will be your fault because you didn't lead them in the way that they needed you to.

You may believe that if they don't produce on their own, then it's their own fault.

Hey, I know the feeling of frustration, probably more so than you do, and I have the same feelings that you do about this, believe me. Most of these people never going to be as talented or driven as you are and fall short of what you think they should be able to do.

But here's the problem.

If you're not able to get enough of these *less-than-perfect* people to produce business, feel good about you as a leader, feel good about your work environment, and if you can't make it easy for them to succeed, they will probably fail.

As much as you know in your heart of hearts that it's not your fault, you have to ask yourself, "What will the end result be if this continues to happen with all of my agents?"

I'll tell you what happens.

You'll have no producers left, no premiums generated, no long-term clients, and you won't have much of an agency.

How do you like the sound of that outcome?

You see, even if you're right, you're the one that ends up suffering. There aren't enough people in this world that are as talented, driven, passionate, and committed as you are.

If you expect your agents to be all of these things at the same level you are, prepare to be disappointed.

The reality is, you should be thankful that they're not as driven as you are. If they were, they'd be building their own agencies – competing against you – not agents at your agency.

Treat your producers like valued business partners, and jump in the trenches with them from time to time. This is how you win over their hearts, and they'll love you in the process.

Now, everything I just explained to you in this chapter so far came from the *First Edition* of this book, which means that this advice came from a 38-year old who was seven years into the insurance game.

Yes, I had accomplished quite a bit at that point, but today I am ten years older and ten years wiser.

I'm also less tolerant of time wasting activities.

Over the last ten years, I have learned two important things:

1. My time has become more valuable and I cannot afford to invest my time in *non-needle moving* activities.
2. Every minute I spend doing *non-needle moving* activities is a minute I could have invested in something more worthwhile.

Back when I wrote the *First Edition* of this book, I had more time to invest in new agents, so I allowed them to waste it. I spent an incredible amount of time trying to drag people across the finish line with me, because my *why* revolved around mentoring people.

I have found there is a distinct difference between mentoring a baby eagle, and wasting time on a pigeon.

Today, I now have five companies instead of one. I now have a 10-year old son. I'm now building companies that are far more sophisticated than my original employee benefits agency.

If I waste time playing grief counselor to a new agent that hasn't generated a dime in profit, it means I'm not spending that time talking to the CEO of a carrier partner, or the Executive Vice-President of one of our twelve banking partners, or an international premium financing client worth $1.2 billion in Asia, or my business partner to develop a new financial platform.

I just don't have the time, patience or tolerance to deal with non-needle moving nonsense.

Part of my *System-Driven Business* is a 221-page agency manual that contains every function, process, rule and decision called *The Playbook*.

Everyone knows this is our agency *Bible*.

Everything is spelled out to the most granular detail.

There is very little that could possibly happen in the universe that couldn't be answered by the contents in *The Playbook*.

"What does Darren think about this?" is a question rarely asked because the answer is already articulated in *The Playbook*, not to mention that I'm now a 7-time published author and many of my books explain how I believe agency tasks should be executed.

I highly recommend that you begin developing your own agency *Playbook*. It is a tedious and painstaking task, and it will probably take you several years to get it dialed in, but now is the time to start.

We also have an administrative *Playbook* with detailed descriptions of how to execute each administrative task imaginable, all the way down to how to set up a new client profile in our CRM system, so if an administrative employee leaves, we have a living document to help train the new replacement.

I also have training videos for new agents. This is a catalogue of well curated live recordings of me doing seminars, webinars and study group trainings. I even have videos and audio recordings of me doing cold-calls and client meetings.

Any training content needed to onboard a new agent is either memorialized in writing (ie: *The Playbook*), or in a video.

In fact, I give all of my people access to a video series called *Checkmate – The Art Of Getting People To Beg You To Tell Them What To Do*, which is a recording of a two-day boot camp seminar I did. This video series breaks down every step of my sales process from A to Z.

I sell this video series on my website at **www.DarrenSugiyama.com**. It contains over nine hours of content.

Is this a shameless plug to get you to go to my website and buy this video series?

Absolutely.

But you'll thank me for it later if you decide to get it. ☺

Okay, back to Rule #2. An important side note about treating your agents like *partners* is that you also have to be fair to yourself.

This can't be a one-way relationship where you are the one always giving and conceding, and your agents are the ones always taking from you and getting their way.

If you're going to treat your agents and the leaders within your organization as *partners*, you must not allow them to treat you like their *Genie In A Bottle*. Often times they get spoiled and expect you to do everything (and pay for everything) for them.

At some point, you need to make a business decision and change the rules of engagement with them if this gets to be a problem.

Compromising never works.

In a compromise, neither party feels good because neither party truly gets what they think they *deserve*, which is the definition of a compromise.

Instead, negotiate a *high-value trade*.

If they want something, give them the *whole enchilada*, under the condition that in exchange, they give you an equally valued *super-deluxe burrito*.

If you only give them *half an enchilada* instead of the *whole enchilada*, they'll feel slighted.

For example, let's say one of your sales team leaders is getting a 3% override, and they're trying to get you to up it to 5%. If you compromise and meet them in the middle at 4%, no matter how successful you are at getting them to concede, they will still feel slighted.

Instead, give them the full 5% under the condition that they start doing something that is of greater or equal value that you want to get off your plate, so you can focus on the bigger needle-moving activities that will generate you more profit than that additional 2% override you gave up.

Of course, this is a completely hypothetical example that may or may not be applicable to your model, but the point is, don't meet halfway in between.

You'll be conceding, and they still won't be happy, which defeats the entire point.

Don't compromise.

Instead, negotiate a *high-value trade*.

Rule #3: Never Criticize Production

Have you ever criticized a sales person for lack of production and had your relationship with them get better?

If you think you have, then you're totally delusional.

Agents do not respond well to criticism in general, but especially not criticism regarding their production numbers.

They get defensive, and ultimately, they'll stop communicating with you.

They will shut down and shut you out, resulting in them eventually leaving your organization.

So how do you get people to see the errors of their ways?

You do this through a two-step process.

Step #1: Teach From Stage.

Teaching From Stage means that you teach certain principles in a group setting, and you focus on the principles, not a particular person. When you're having a group staff meeting or when you're doing an agent training with multiple agents, you can criticize certain types of behavior without criticizing specific people.

You can be a real hard-ass when it comes to criticizing *behavior* in a group setting, so for all you hard-asses out there, here's your chance.

Be a total hard-ass when it comes to being adamant about how to run your business process and system, but do it *from stage*, and never, ever, ever criticize individual agent's production numbers.

So how do you address an agent's lack of performance?

You have them self-evaluate.

Step #2: Have Your Agents Self-Evaluate.

You should have quarterly, one-on-one progress meetings with your agents to discuss their performance, but here's the key: Never criticize them.

All you want to do is review their numbers.

That's why it's so important to track both activity results and production results.

You've got to have a business system where you and your producers agree on a production goal.

Let them set their own goals when it comes to production. Remember, they're an independent contractor, which means they're technically in business for themselves. You are a *resource* for them to amplify their production, which should amplify your agency's profit as well.

Once they tell you what their production goals are, plug their numbers into the *Electronic Truth Teller* and allow it to serve as the basis of your discussion. It will reveal to them what they have to do to hit their financial goals.

The beauty of this process is that *they* are the ones that set their production goals, not *you*. This means that they're taking ownership of their production goals, and you are perceived as the mentor that is helping them attain these goals for their benefit, not yours.

Once you're in this role, your people will trust you more. This is the type of relationship you want to develop with them.

Once these goals are set and the action plan is put in place, the one-on-one self-evaluation meeting is easy, which is where step two comes in.

Have them tell you about their activity level and their production for the quarter (you should both be looking at the same production report print out), and ask them, "So how do you *feel* about your numbers?"

Notice, I didn't say, "How do you feel about how things are going."

I specifically asked them how they feel about their *numbers*.

Here's what happens.

If they're hitting their production goal, they get to tell you the good news. They get to tell you how well they're doing and how they're tracking perfectly.

This is like a kid coming home with a report card to show his parents he's getting straight A's. It's a time of celebration and validation, and you get to congratulate them.

They're seeking your approval, and you're giving it to them. This makes them feel proud and empowers them.

Now, if they're not hitting their numbers, they already know it. Having you scold them for it isn't going to help the cause. That's what's so great about having them focus on their production reports. They can't escape the numbers, and the numbers don't lie.

When you review their production numbers together and you ask them how they feel about their numbers, they'll criticize themselves.

They already know they're messing up.

Just listen to them.

They're probably embarrassed, and they're expecting you to criticize them, so they're already filled with anxiety.

When you don't criticize them and you just listen to them, they feel like you're being supportive, and therefore trust is built on a deeper level.

You must keep the lines of communication open with your people, always.

When you let them self-evaluate, they're going to be harder on themselves than you were going to be on them, which is exactly what you want.

They'll tell you what they're doing wrong, and they'll ask you for advice.

This is an opportunity for you to coach them and recalibrate their approach. Again, they're empowered by this process because they're the ones that are setting their goals.

Just listen to them and be supportive because the reality is they're going to do whatever they're going to do, regardless. You might as well make them feel like you've got their back.

But here's where the real magic happens.

This type of one-on-one meeting ends with you asking them, "What part of your game do you feel you need the most help with?"

Sometimes it's going to be closing.

Sometimes it's going to be overcoming objections.

Whatever the issue is, if you have a *System-Driven Business*, you've taught a training session on this topic before.

Instead of just giving them the answer, ask them this brief series of questions:

1. Do you remember the training I did on this topic?
2. So, what adjustments do you think you need to make?
3. What do you think is the best way to implement this?

In most cases, they already know the answer. If they come up blank, then just reteach that topic right there on the spot.

If they do happen to give you the right answer, then just smile and say, "See, you already know the answer. Man, I've trained you well!"

This should elicit a chuckle of relief from them.

The reason this type of *teaching through discovery* is so powerful is that it reinforces the fact that your business systems are that great.

You've already taught them these principles because you foresaw these issues coming up before they actually came up.

You're now perceived as a visionary because you've already been through the exact same thing they're going through, so you're relatable to them.

A great leader must be relatable to the common man. You must reinforce the fact that you are all-powerful while at the same time reminding your people that you started out just like them, so you *get* where they're at.

The minute your people feel that you've lost touch, they will lose respect for you, and they won't want to follow you into battle anymore.

If they feel like you're right there in the trenches with them and that you understand what they're going through, they'll be loyal ambassadors of your brand and great partners.

Now you've built trust with your people.

They know what they're supposed to be doing.

If they're not doing what they're supposed to be doing, they're aware of it, and they know you're aware of it.

The question is, "How do you get people into action that aren't currently producing on a consistent basis?"

Obviously, ragging on them doesn't work, and using guilt never works long-term.

This leads us to rule four: *Create Internal Jealousy* within your agency.

Rule #4: Create Internal Positive Jealousy

This probably sounds odd to you.

You must understand human behavioral patterns to really understand why this is so effective.

Jealousy is one of the strongest emotions human beings have. Jealousy can drive us to do things that we normally wouldn't do. Jealous husbands have murdered their wives. Jealous wives have cut off their husbands' body parts. Remember Lorena Bobbitt?

Jealousy is a powerful emotion.

You need to use this human emotion to your advantage, especially when it comes to installing a new system or methodology into your agency.

In the past, whenever I used to come up with a new, brilliant idea, I would roll it out to all of my producers, and initially, only about 10% to 20% of them would embrace it and put it into action.

The others would be very resistant to a new way of doing things. Surprise, surprise.

That's just the way human beings are. It used to frustrate the hell out of me.

So what did I do?

I tried using guilt.

I used to practically browbeat people into submission.

I used to try to force them to do things my way.

Guess what the end result was.

I got people to do things my way for a week or two, and they begrudgingly did it because I said so, but after a couple of weeks, they went right back to doing things their old way.

To make matters worse, not only did their actions not change permanently, but they also resented me for forcing them to do things my way.

Nobody won in this battle, especially not me.

I finally came up with a better strategy.

I tapped into the power of creating *Internal Jealousy*.

Here's how this strategy works.

Whenever you come up with a new, brilliant strategy, roll it out to two of your key agents.

You have to make sure you have a strong enough relationship with these two agents. They must understand that new ideas require testing, and quite frankly, these particular two agents must *love* the process of trying new things.

If your test pilot bombs, no problem.

No one knew it ever existed with the exception of you and your two pilot agents.

Most people don't understand the process of testing, and if they see two or more new ideas fail, they'll never be open to any new ideas ever again.

I see this happen in sales organizations all the time.

After a series of failed new programs, whenever the organization launches their new *Best Idea Ever*, it's perceived as just another *flavor-of-the-month* gimmick.

That's why you must test new ideas for at least four to six weeks before you roll them out to the masses.

Now, if your new strategy tests well, you're going to brag about your results to everyone. Talk about how much new business this new strategy is producing. Talk about how much money your key guys are making using this new strategy.

Here's what will happen.

Everyone else will get jealous. They'll want the same results your test pilot guys are getting, which means they'll be begging you for your new secret strategy.

When this happens, you've created *Internal Positive Jealousy*.

Once this happens, you won't need to *force* your people to do things your way.

It's just the opposite.

They'll be begging you to teach them your new strategy.

Mission accomplished.

You now have virtually 100% buy-in from your agents without even trying, because eventually, their jealousy of the superior results using the new strategy will override their resistance to change, and it will be a proven, indisputable fact that the new strategy is superior.

Either way, you (and everyone in your agency) will win, which is exactly what you want.

Creating *Internal Positive Jealousy* makes your people come to you, producing gratitude, loyalty, and ultimately, millions of dollars.

What I've Learned Over The Last 10 Years About Mentoring & Developing Agents

As I mentioned earlier in this chapter, the value I put on my time has drastically changed over the last decade.

All of my original *rules* as it pertains to running a crew of 1099 agents still apply today. Everything in this chapter is as relevant today as it was ten years ago, but I am in a different phase of my business and my personal life now.

The one big thing I failed to articulate in the *First Edition* of this chapter was how to deal with sub-leaders in your organization.

My old model was to build sub-teams within my agency.

Here are the problems I encountered with that model.

The superstar agent would earn themselves a *Senior Agent* position, and I would stack new agents onto their team. The new agents would book meetings into the *Senior Agent's* calendar. The *Senior Agent* would close the deal, and the two would do a commission split.

It was great for the new *Junior Agent* because they could rely on the *Senior Agent's* experience and closing ability. It was great for the *Senior Agent* because they had a full calendar and had no concerns regarding lead generation.

It all made sense in theory.

Here's where it went sideways.

The *Senior Agents* got massive egos. They started treating the new agents like they were their subordinate employees. The new agents despised them for being treated like this.

In addition, we wanted to grow exponentially. We had so many new agents coming onboard that we *had* to promote good agents into *Senior Agent* roles before they were truly ready.

At one point, some of our *Senior Agents* were running teams of 20+ agents, which was way too many *Junior Agents* for one *Senior Agent* to manage. We started growing *wide* too fast because we couldn't grow any *deeper*.

The *Senior Agents* were closing a ton of business in terms of volume, but their closing percentage was not great. As an example, if a *Senior Agent* was getting fed appointments by 20 agents, if they just close one deal per agent per month, that's 20 clients per month for the *Senior Agent*, which was great for the *Senior Agent*, but that meant each of the *Junior Agents* were only winning over one client per month, which they couldn't survive on.

When I tried to explain this to the *Senior Agents*, they resisted my coaching because selfishly, things were working out great for them. They didn't understand that the most important life blood of a growing agency is to make our new people successful so they stay and multiply.

So the *Junior Agents* would quit because the *Senior Agents* weren't closing enough deals for them. When the *Senior Agent's* team dwindled, they expected me to stack more agents on their team. They hadn't done their own prospecting for so long, they felt they were above it, so they blamed me for not continuing to build their team for them. I call this *Senioritis*.

On top of that, since they were 1099s as well, I couldn't force them to start prospecting on their own. So all of a sudden, I had to shoulder the responsibility and accept the blame for not being able to pull rabbits out of my hat every single week.

These agents got spoiled, felt entitled and became lazy.

To add an additional layer of complexity on top of that, some of them had *override* deals with me, so as they stopped grinding it out, they kept getting paid on new business being generated by the agents that no longer needed them to close for them.

But that wasn't even the main problem.

The main problem was that I was the one grinding it out still, and they were coasting, benefiting by riding on my coat tails. They were neglecting their responsibilities to assist the agents that could close business on their own, but still needed their guidance. Essentially, they were getting paid to be an absentee faux-mentor. So guess who had to do all the work, picking up their slack? Me.

So what did I do?

I became bitter, angry and resentful.

Young agents making 6-figures due to my systems were now spoiled and entitled, complaining about the very system that made them successful in the first place. It was then when I realized I needed to change my mindset, develop a new business model, and a operate from a brand new perspective.

CHAPTER 10

NEW PERSPECTIVE

Empires are rarely destroyed by opposing empires.

They are usually destroyed from within.

Betrayals and *coup d'é·tats* are often led by the people the leader helped the most, which is why the saying *No Good Deed Goes Unpunished* exists.

Every successful person I know has gone through a massive betrayal whether it was in business or in their personal life.

When this happens, we search for answers to the question, "Why do bad things happen to good people?"

Every time I've experienced a betrayal or had someone leave my organization, I would later discover that it was a blessing in disguise.

As I said at the beginning of this book, sometimes the people that start out with you aren't necessarily the ones that continue with you, especially when it's time for you to elevate to the next level.

This is not a bad thing.

It may be painful, but it is for your own benefit.

You must change your mindset from being resentful that these things happened *to* you, to being grateful that these things happened *for* you.

I realize this is much easier said than done.

Everyone has their own process of mentally and emotionally coping with betrayals and setbacks.

For me, I find my power in another F-word: *Faith.*

You don't have to be a religious or spiritual person to understand what *faith* is.

You exhibit *faith* in your life every day.

When you drive down a two-lane highway, you trust that the car driving in the opposite lane is going to stay in their lane and not cause a head-on collision with you.

This is a form of *faith*.

Simply put, *faith* is choosing to believe in something you cannot see and cannot prove – trusting that something will or will not happen – despite there being no guarantee.

Every entrepreneur exhibits this same type of faith in their daily business operations, because in the world of business, there are clearly no guarantees.

But when we are betrayed, our faith in people often times suffers as we search for answers that are difficult to find.

Friedrich Nietzsche said, "To live is to suffer, to survive is to find meaning in the suffering."

I truly believe that if you can make sense of challenges and hardships – to find the *meaning* in the suffering – then you can create a platform to not only survive, but grow exponentially as a person in the areas of perseverance, wisdom and discernment.

If the *meaning* behind your shortstop leaving was to make room for Derek Jeter to step into that position on your team, you would be celebrating their departure.

I have found two things to be universally true in this regard:

1. Higher-quality people will only come into your life once you remove the toxic people.
2. If you're too stubborn to remove the toxic people yourself, sometimes God does it for you.

Though having people leave you can be a very painful experience, remember what I said earlier. No one has ever said, "I wish that jackass was still on my team."

If you are currently experiencing a betrayal, embrace their decision to leave because a higher-caliber person can now fill that void.

Every incredible relationship I have in my life today came on the heels of a painful departure of a previous relationship.

When you are dealing with the aftermath of being betrayed – whether these challenges be emotional, financial, or both – it is easy to become resentful and bitter.

It is also easy to become anxious and fearful about how all of this will affect your future.

Have you ever had feelings of despair and stress about the future, or resentment and bitterness about the past?

The Past

When you have feelings of resentment, bitterness and insecurity, these are feelings associated with your *past*.

Any resentment or bitterness you may be currently feeling is due to what someone said or did to you months or even years ago.

Additionally, any insecurities you may currently have are rooted in negative experiences from your past that made you feel unaccepted or *not good enough* and may stretch as far back as your childhood.

Whatever negative feelings you may be feeling in the present are usually linked to things that have happened to you in the past.

The Future

When you have feelings of anxiety, worry and fear, these are feelings associated with your *future*.

You may find yourself feeling anxious or fearful about what might happen in the future, worrying about things that haven't happened yet.

Any angst about the future is usually triggered by your perspective on your current situation. If you are dissatisfied with your current state of affairs – specifically in the area of an unfulfilled *want* – it is only natural that you would fear that things may continue as they have with your desired outcome never coming into fruition.

The Present

When you have feelings of gratitude, these are feelings associated with the *present*.

When you are in a state of ultimate gratitude, it is literally impossible to simultaneously feel anger, resentment or bitterness because everything that has happened in your past – both pleasurable and painful experiences – is now redefined as being responsible for the positive outcome that you are currently grateful for.

This perspective forces you to rationalize that all the heartaches, struggles and hardships were necessary elements that made your current situation possible.

Thus, if you are grateful for your present situation, then you must also be grateful for your past, regardless of how painful it may have been, for it is your past that is responsible for your present. So if you want to rid yourself of anger, bitterness and resentment, focus on what you are grateful for today, and you will experience an entire recontextualization of your past.

Gratitude also rids yourself of anxiety, worry and fear. As I have already discussed, these are feelings associated with the *future*.

Angst about the future is usually due to wanting something to happen in the future so badly that the mere thought of it not happening makes you upset in the present.

Typically it is the dissatisfaction of your current situation that gives you angst about the future because you have bought into the lie that life's progression is linear and that the trajectory of your life up until this point will continue in a straight line with no exponential possibilities.

But when you are in a state of *ultimate gratitude* in the present, you feel complete and full because you realize that you have far more than what you previously recognized.

This realization makes you appreciate your past without resentment, and gives you peace about your future without fear.

I am blessed to have a small group of amazing friends that understand the power of gratitude, and when we talk, almost every conversation ends with us talking about what we are grateful for.

Just yesterday, I had a conversation with one of my best friends who is also an entrepreneur. We discussed how our marketing strategies continue to evolve, especially in the midst of this COVID-19 environment.

Of course there are challenges that a pandemic brings into the business world, however we spent the majority of the time talking about how we are finding new opportunities in the midst of this chaos and uncertainty, as well as what we are grateful for.

We discussed how grateful we are for the lessons we've learned by going through past struggles and how that pain has made us tougher. We discussed how fortunate we are to be rid of past business partners and certain employees. We discussed how fortunate we are to be married to strong, wise women and how blessed we are to have happy, healthy children.

Think about the majority of conversations you have with people for a moment.

How much of those conversations are focused on gratitude, versus blaming, complaining and gossiping about others?

If you could change the content of these conversations to being more focused on gratitude, what do you think would happen to your mindset?

If your mindset was centered around being grateful for the lessons you've learned from past challenging experiences and excitement about the possibilities that your future holds, what affect would that have on your ability to perform?

You would become an unstoppable warrior.

You would become a leader worth following.

So how can you install this mindset of gratitude?

An easy way to begin your self-installation of this mindset is to pick just one thing you're thankful for but often times take for granted.

Let's say it's your children's health.

It is difficult to explicitly visualize and internalize this exercise, but take a moment and think about how much you love your children.

Now imagine you find out that one of your children just got diagnosed with Stage 4 leukemia.

You are devasted, but you put on a brave face for your child.

They undergo chemotherapy, but the doctor informs you that the treatments aren't working.

Your child loses all of their hair. They become weak and frail, vomiting in the toilet bowl repeatedly every night. They are afraid.

They look at you with tears in their eyes and ask you, "Mommy, Daddy, am I going to die?"

You are completely distraught. After a few weeks, the doctor pulls you and your spouse into a private room.

He says, "Unfortunately, we need a bone marrow transplant in order for your child to survive and we need it soon, but finding a match is very difficult."

"How much time do we have?" you ask.

"Three to four weeks, maybe less," the doctor says.

Just let this sink in for a moment. Try to put yourself in that exact situation. Thousands of parents have been in this situation before, so this is not an impossibility for any of us to face. It could literally happen to any of us, at any time.

Now imagine, one week goes by. Then two weeks.

Three weeks, and still no donor match is found.

Your child looks at you and says, "It's okay mommy. It's okay daddy. It's not your fault. Maybe it's my time to go to heaven now."

You fight to hold tears back and attempt to give your child some encouraging words, but there have been zero prospects of finding a bone marrow donor match thus far.

You are now in your fourth week. Still no donor match.

One night you are at home sleeping in your bed, feeling guilty for not spending every moment in the hospital by your child's side.

Then your phone rings. It's the doctor.

"We found a match, but we need you to come to the hospital right away. We don't have much time," the doctor says.

You rush to the hospital, and by the time you get there, the doctor is already in his scrubs. Your child is barely hanging on, and the donor is already in the operating room, ready for the bone marrow transplant.

As you and your spouse wait anxiously in the waiting room, you fidget with your phone as your balmy hands cannot hold the phone steady.

You catch glimpses of your spouse's facial expressions, but you're too nervous to look them in the eyes.

One hour goes by. Then two.

The doctor suddenly appears and approaches you.

"I'm sorry to keep you so long. We had some issues with the extraction, so we're not certain how your child's body is going to accept the transplant," the doctor says.

Each morning, you wake up and walk into your child's room, praying that you'll see their chest rising and falling as they sleep peacefully.

Day after day.

Week after week.

Month after month.

You eagerly anticipate your child's lab results to be reviewed by the doctor at each check-up, and one day, the doctor tells you, "We are 100% cancer-free. I think a celebration is in order!"

You reach out to your child's donor and invite them to a special party to celebrate your child's recovery.

When they walk in the door to your home, you hug them, sobbing uncontrollably, and can't seem to let go. You are filled with so much gratitude, nothing else matters in this moment.

When you look into your child's eyes, you fully understand what that kind of loss would have meant, and the gratitude you feel in your heart is beyond anything you have ever experienced before.

You no longer take your child's health for granted because you have redefined it as a *gift*, not an *expectation*.

Recontextualizing Your Present

Often times it takes going through a traumatic experience that ends in a glorious outcome in order to realize how blessed we are, but it doesn't need to be this way.

You are experiencing several miracles right now.

If your child is currently healthy, that is a miracle.

If you can walk, that is also a miracle.

The problem is that because you have become accustomed to these miracles, you take them for granted. This is your *current normal*, and as we discussed earlier, it is easy to take your *new normal* and your *current normal* for granted.

Unless you take the time to go through the exercise of visualizing what your life would be like if these blessings were taken away from you, they are often times taken for granted.

But if you can connect with what I'm saying here and truly appreciate what you have, you will then enter a state of ultimate gratitude.

This is the only time you will ever truly feel *complete*.

You won't focus so much on what you *don't* have because you are too busy focusing on being grateful for what you *do* have.

Now, perhaps you're reading this and you're thinking to yourself, "This sounds pretty hippie-schmippie to me."

Rest assured, it is not.

This is not just a spiritual thing, nor is it esoteric.

This is a scientifically-proven phenomenon that human beings experience at the biochemical level.

The Science Of Happiness

Most people's happiness is simply linked to pleasure and pain.

They have an experience and if it is pleasurable, they are happy. If it is painful, they are unhappy.

It's actually a little more complex than that.

Our body's biochemistry has a direct cause-and-effect relationship with our happiness and emotional well-being.

For example, *dopamine* is a hormone and neurotransmitter that your brain produces to send messages between nerve cells and plays a major role in how you *feel*.

Dopamine gives you instant pleasure and the feeling of *happiness*.

When you receive a *like* on a social media post, or when you buy a new outfit, or when you see someone you're sexually attracted to, you will experience a surge in production of dopamine.

You experience an emotional *high*.

The problem however is that with all things that give you a *high*, they are addictive, and over time, your *high* becomes your *new normal*.

In order to create that same level of emotional ecstasy, you need an even more extreme experience to get the same dopamine hit, and as your pleasure threshold becomes higher and higher, you become similar to an addict that can't get *high* anymore.

What used to give you pleasure is not pleasurable enough anymore, so you continue to chase that same *high* you once experienced by pursuing something bigger and better, never able to fully quench that thirst.

You become a *dopamine fiend*.

Think about every *high* you've ever gotten from buying a new car, or a new watch or piece of jewelry, or a new pair of shoes.

How long did that *high* last before it was replaced by feelings of dissatisfaction and wanting something new?

Ladies, you probably have an entire closet full of nothing to wear. Men, the car you're currently sick of driving was once your dream car. This is further proof that a purchase that once made you so happy is either collecting dust in your closet, or is not cool enough to drive anymore.

Coming to this realization has largely influenced my brand overhaul. Though there is nothing wrong with enjoying nice things, when the pursuit of nice things becomes the focus, it is not so different than a drug addict chasing the high they will never get.

No matter how many toys you buy, you will never be satisfied because every new toy you buy quickly loses its luster, leaving you feeling empty and wanting a new shiny object.

You become the proverbial *hamster on the wheel*.

Your goal should never be *happiness*.

Your goal should be gratitude and *ultimate joy*.

The Science Of Gratitude & Ultimate Joy

A close-but-different cousin to *dopamine* is *oxytocin*.

Oxytocin is a hormone secreted by the pituitary gland in the brain and is known as the *bonding hormone*. Its production is triggered when you cuddle with a loved one, or when a mother holds her newborn to her chest.

A study was done wherein female rats that had previously given birth to a litter of pups were injected with oxytocin, and then surrounded by baby rats that were not hers. In these tests, the mama rat bonded with the pups as if they were her own.

However, when virgin female rats were subjected to the same oxytocin injection and the same foreign pups, studies found that such virgin female rats did not bond with the pups in the same way that the mothers that had once given birth did.

This study led scientists to believe that oxytocin only triggered emotional responses of bonding when linked to a positive past experience – in this case, motherhood.

A similar test was done with male human beings in which dads who got a boost of *oxytocin* via a nasal spray played more closely with their 5-month old babies than dads from the same focus group who did not receive the oxytocin nasal spray.

In addition, another study was published in the *Proceedings of the National Academy of Sciences of the United States of America (PNAS)* in 2010 wherein men were administered a dose of *oxytocin* prior to them describing their relationships with their mothers.

Those with healthy, positive mother-son relationships described their moms as being more caring after the *oxytocin* hit. But the men that had troublesome relationships with their mothers described their moms as being less caring.

This study found that *oxytocin* seemed to intensify past social and familial memories, whether positive or negative.

So why am I going into all of this?

Because when you are in a state of gratitude, your brain naturally surges in *oxytocin* production.

When you are focused on being grateful in the present for something that happened in your past, you can change your neuro-association with that past experience from negative to positive, and also form a new positive emotional bond with such event.

This is one way to cathartically work through the demons from your past.

If you rewire your brain to look at those hurtful experiences as necessary building blocks that have made you a better person, you can free yourself from the emotional prison of your past.

But it doesn't stop there.

*Oxytoci*n signals something called *Endothelium-Derived Relaxing Factor (EDRF)*.

Scientist Robert F. Furchgott won a *Nobel Prize in Medicine* in 1998 for his research findings regarding *EDRF*.

His research proved that *EDRF* – being an endogenous vasodilator – caused vascular smooth muscle to relax. The cardiac muscle of your heart is one of these vascular smooth muscles.

This muscle tissue contracts and releases involuntarily and is responsible for pumping blood throughout your body. The *EDRF* relaxes this cardiac muscle tissue, and as its blood vessels dilate, your heart becomes engorged with blood.

You essentially get a heart-on.

Ironically enough, this research was used in the development of the drug *Viagra*.

With a more muscularly-relaxed, blood-engorged heart, your heart is literally full – full of blood.

When you hear phrases like, "My heart feels so full," or "I'm full of joy," these aren't just metaphors.

These are physiological descriptions of what involuntarily happens to your heart during feelings of extreme gratitude.

Your heart becomes full of blood, and you become full of joy.

So why is this relevant to your insurance business?

If you can proactively install this process into your conscious mind and elevate your awareness of what you have to be grateful for, it will eventually become engraved in your subconscious, becoming your new default emotional reaction.

But if you do not install this mindset, you will be a slave to your current default method of processing challenging experiences, which is one of victimization and defeat.

When you experience times of sorrow, stress or challenge, it is easy to slip into your default emotional loop:

1. Challenging event is associated with a negative meaning.
2. Negative meaning triggers a negative biochemical reaction.

3. Negative biochemical reaction triggers a negative emotion.
4. Negative emotion triggers a negative action.
5. Negative action creates a negative outcome.

So how do you interrupt this pattern?

The first step of breaking this pattern and reprograming a new emotional roadmap is to first understand how this negative emotional loop came to be.

Understanding Negative Emotional Loops

Your brain's default emotional program is rooted in an innate survival mechanism that is hardwired into your neurological system.

When you experience a threatening event, the emotional feeling of *fear* is generated in a part of your brain called the amygdala. Once the amygdala generates the emotion of fear, it signals impulses to another part of your brain called the hypothalamus. The hypothalamus then signals impulses to the rest of your body to prepare for a fight-or-flight response.

This is an involuntary biochemical response that both humans and animals have to increase their chances of survival in potentially threatening situations. In nature, organisms with the strongest flight-or-fight responses increase their species chance of survival.

The emotions associated with fear cause your adrenal glands to produce *epinephrine* (also called adrenaline) causing an increase in heart rate and the energy to either fight or run.

However despite the fact that you don't live in the jungle and you aren't being chased by a Tyrannosaurus Rex, this hormonal response is hardwired into your system and is programmed to run involuntarily.

When people say, "I can't control how I feel," it is because their innate survival system triggers biochemical hormonal surges, which signal emotions. These survival-based emotions are helpful when being chased by a hungry T-Rex, but not very conducive to governing business decisions.

In addition, events from your past that triggered the most intense emotional reactions have engraved an *emotional memory* in your conscious mind. The longer the refractory period of this memory and the emotions associated with it last, the more your emotional memory becomes permanently engraved in your subconscious mind.

If this refractory period lasts for more than a few days, it becomes your *mood*.

If it lasts for more than a few months, it becomes your *temperament*.

If it lasts for more than a year, it can become your *permanent disposition* because once it is engraved in your subconscious mind, it becomes part of who you are. This is extremely detrimental in making wise decisions in both your business life and your personal life.

When you encounter a bitter person with a toxic personality, it is usually the result of an extended refractory period after they experienced something negative, which created their unpleasant disposition.

So how do you prevent this from happening to you?

When you experience a challenging event, your brain recalls past challenging events in order to put the new challenging event into context, which triggers the amygdala to produce the feeling of fear. This is where the negative emotional chain reaction typically begins.

The key to preventing this negative inertia from causing your brain to continually run your default emotional program is to intervene and shorten the refractory period of your negative emotion.

You may not be able to control how you initially feel when confronted with a challenging event in your life, but you can certainly control how you process that initial feeling to shorten the refractory period.

Here's how your brain typically processes events:

An event occurs and your brain contextualizes the event by searching its memory for a similar past event. Your brain then attaches meaning to the new event. The meaning causes your brain to create a biochemical reaction. The biochemical reaction creates an emotion. The emotion creates a thought. The thought triggers an action. Your action produces an outcome, which you attach meaning to... and the cycle continues. This is your default emotional loop.

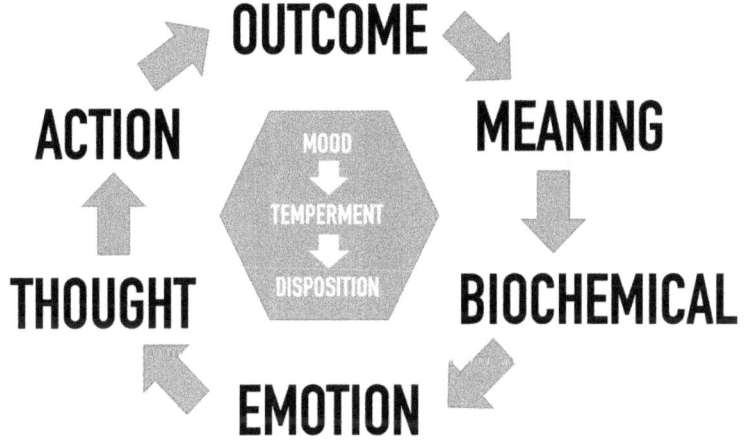

Although you cannot control your emotions, you can control your thoughts about your emotions.

This is called *metacognition* – the awareness and understanding of one's own thought process.

You can also control the way you recontextualize past events, changing their meaning to create new emotions associated with those past events.

So if you can change the meaning of your past and change the meaning of a current outcome, you have the power to break this default emotional loop and recalibrate it.

Through metacognition, you can attach a new meaning to the outcome – one that is positive instead of negative. Perhaps the *meaning* of the outcome is that a bigger opportunity exists for you – that one door closed in order for a bigger one to open.

If you entered a state of gratitude for this *blessing in disguise*, your hypothalamus would signal oxytocin, creating the feeling of joy and certainty. This emotional state would be conducive to creating an innovative needle-moving strategy, allowing you to make a power play that results in you dominating your industry.

How's that for an outcome?

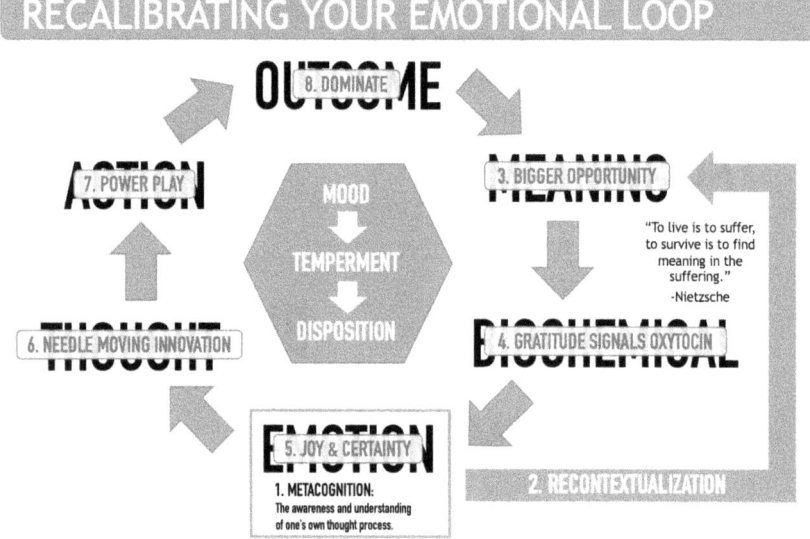

You must change your brain's default emotional program from being a *record of your past*, to a *road map to your future*.

This can be done through meditation.

The Science Of Meditation

Since you cannot control your emotions, learning how to control your *thoughts* about your emotions is what meditation is all about. If you can control your thoughts about your emotions – to understand their meaning – you can recontextualize past events and present circumstances.

If you do this successfully, you can control your brain's involuntary biochemical response to your experiences, which ultimately controls your emotions.

This is how you can change your entire disposition from being a *fearful person* to being a *confident person* – from being a *pessimist* to an *optimist*.

You can literally rewire your brain's biochemical proclivity.

I happen to do this through meditation.

I'm not talking about smoking ayahuasca in a hot teepee, or chanting, "auuuuuuuummmmm" while sitting cross-legged on a mountain top with my thumbs lightly touching my ring fingers (not that there's anything wrong with either of these things – I'm not judging other people's rituals).

Meditation is simply taking some quiet time to become aware of your thoughts and consciously attach different meanings to them.

The origin of the word *meditate* comes from the Latin word *meditārī*, which means to *reflect upon*.

The more consciously aware you are of your thoughts and feelings, the less likely you are to fall back into the unconscious repetition of your default negative emotional cycle.

You can literally program a new positive emotional cycle to become your default method of processing events, as well as your feelings about these events.

Over time, the same positive thoughts will create the same positive behaviors. Positive behaviors tend to create positive outcomes. Positive outcomes create positive emotions. Positive emotions create positive thoughts… and the cycle continues.

My meditation process is just simply sitting quietly with my eyes closed as I reflect upon what I am grateful for.

First, I reflect upon three relationships that I'm most grateful for at that moment.

These three relationships change from session to session, for I certainly have more than just three relationships in my life to be grateful for. If you are similar to me in this regard, this alone is a huge indicator that your circumstance is not as bad as you may feel it is in that moment.

But even if you only have ONE relationship to be thankful for in your life, there are people in this world that would give their right arm to have one relationship as valuable as the one you have. The intent here is to focus on what you *have*, because your default emotional program tends to focus on what you *don't have*.

These are three examples of my most valued relationships that I am grateful for:

Relationships I'm Grateful For (1-3):

1. My marriage. My wife has given me wise counsel both in my personal life and in my business life. She encourages me in times of struggle. She celebrates me in times of success. She treats my friends as if they were her own brothers. She is my best friend and most trusted advisor.

    My wife is an amazing mother to our son. She has greatly contributed to his confidence and made him feel secure. She is a great disciplinarian, yet nurturing at the same time. Our son's beautiful spirit is a reflection of my wife.

    I am grateful that God sent me the wife He knew I needed.

2. My relationship with my son. Every Thursday and Friday night, my 10-year old son and I spend the night in our guest room. We have our weekly father-and-son talk during this time where we talk about everything from friendships, girls and serious issues, to silly things like watches and cars.

    My son is kind, generous and thoughtful. He has compassion towards others and understands the value of loyalty, integrity and honor. I am proud of the person he is and the man he is in the process of becoming.

    I am grateful for the type of relationship we have.

3. <u>My current business partner, Jeff.</u> Our partnership is the first business partnership I've ever had where I never have to worry about him contributing as much value as I do, which is saying a lot.

   We've become like brothers over the past few years, and I couldn't do what I'm doing in business right now without him, which again, is saying a lot.

   Our values are aligned, our skillsets complement each other, his work ethic is just as obsessive as mine, and I am grateful to God for sending him into my life. He is a great business partner, great friend and great man.

Of course there are many other relationships I am thankful for which regularly get inserted into rotation during these sessions, but these are just three examples of them.

In addition to people, there are past experiences and present situations I am grateful for as well. I choose to focus on these three things as my blessings #4, #5 and #6.

<u>Experiences I'm Grateful For (4-6):</u>

4. I will think of something that happened that seemed to be negative at first, but ended up resulting in something positive.

   Sometimes things happen and we think they are setbacks, but later in life as we are able to connect the dots, we realize they were set-ups for something greater to happen for us.

   Notice I said *for* us, not *to* us.

   As you begin to do this more and more, you will soon realize that practically everything negative that has happened to you in your life has turned into a blessing.

   Not only does this make you more grateful for your present situation, but it also gives you a new understanding of how to frame future experiences that appear to be negative on the surface, for you now associate doors shutting with better alternative doors opening.

5. Next I will meditate on a chance encounter with someone that logically should not have happened (or at least could have easily not happened), and how this encounter changed my life for the better.

What seemed to be a total coincidence ended up being a divine intervention.

Some of my new relationships that appeared be initiated by a random chance encounter were not random at all. They were gifts, and I am thankful for them.

6. Lastly, I will meditate on a current opportunity I have in front of me that I was coincidentally exposed to. This will change from time to time because I always have so many business projects I'm simultaneously working on.

Again, the mere exercise of realizing you have so many things to be thankful for that you struggle to decide which one you focus on is a great reminder of how blessed you really are.

I used to take a lot of credit for *manifesting* business opportunities, but once I realized that a certain chain of events had to happen (which I had no control or influence over) in order to make certain opportunities open up for me, I became acutely aware that these were *blessings*, not *self-manifestations*.

What we do with these opportunities is largely up to us, but the opportunities themselves are gifts given to us, and deserving of our gratitude.

During this meditative practice, I will envision this current opportunity coming into fruition. I will allow myself to feel the emotions of what my desired outcome would feel like, being grateful for not only the outcome, but also for the opportunity that was given to me.

What makes this meditation practice so powerful for me is that I used to feel like my whole life was about overcoming bad luck and misfortune.

Embarrassingly I must admit, I was a martyr.

This is a terrible perspective on life for two reasons:

1. It reinforces the belief that the world is against you, and that the universe does not want you to win. This belief alone limits the blessings you are able to receive simply because you have negative expectations, resulting a victim mentality.
2. It allows your ego to believe that when you overcome this bad luck, that you are 100% responsible for the outcome.

It is nearly impossible to be grateful when you think the universe is against you. It is also nearly impossible to have humility when you take 100% credit for every positive outcome.

When you focus on these three special people and these three special blessings in the context which I just explained, you become aware that you did nothing to deserve these blessings. They happened *for you*.

It is important to recognize this and take inventory of how often these things have happened *for you*.

Two things become very apparent in this exercise:

1. You realize how many things you have to be grateful for.
2. You realize how much good fortune you have been blessed with outside of your own efforts.

This simple meditation only takes about 15-20 minutes per day, but just like working out, it is easy to not do. It takes a real commitment and obsessive discipline to carve out the time to do these types of things.

But this *practice* is no less important than writing a great script, or developing a brilliant *PowerPoint*, or forming a powerful business alliance.

Similar to prayer, we often times only surrender to this type of practice when we are humbled by a devasting setback. But you don't have wait for a setback to occur to reap the benefits of meditation right now.

Let meditation be your first action, not your last resort.

For me, my gratitude is rooted in my relationship with God, but you don't need to share my spiritual and religious beliefs to benefit from this practice.

You can be a 100% science-based atheist and still believe in the undeniable neuroscientific effects of gratitude and its relation to the body's production of oxytocin, as well as Furchgott's Nobel Prize winning findings regarding *Endothelium-Derived Relaxing Factor (EDRF)*.

Regardless of your spiritual beliefs, if you approach life with a heart of gratitude, you will have a level of relaxed confidence that sets you apart from everyone else.

You won't feel desperate and won't appear thirsty.

You won't live your life in reactionary mode being controlled and victimized by the events around you.

You will have a level of certainty that no matter what happens in life, you know will be just fine.

Imagine how powerful you would become if you had this level of certainty.

This requires an overhaul in your recollection of past experiences, the meaning you attach to them, and how you intervene and disrupt your default emotional program.

Programming The Subconscious Mind

Studies have shown that the subconscious mind cannot decipher the difference between an experience that is responsible for an emotion, versus an emotion that is created by thought alone.

What this means is that the mere visualization of something happening gives the subconscious mind the illusionary experience that the event is actually happening because it experiences the same emotion.

Since it cannot decipher the difference between the emotion and the actual event, your body creates the hormones and biochemistry as if the visualized event has actually happened.

For example, if your brain has involuntarily created oxytocin which leads to EDRF, you would biochemically experience the emotion of joy.

If this practice is repeated consistently over time, you might just start walking around feeling joyful and confident all day long, every day. This installation of *neurological software* could literally become your new *neurological hardware*, meaning you could literally create a new version of yourself.

Your disposition, personality traits and confidence level would be that of a successful and joyful person.

And how do you think other people would respond to you if exuded this type of authentic confidence created by neuroscience?

People would be drawn to you like a magnet.

This is not *fake-it-till-you-make-it* posturing.

This is literally changing your involuntary hormonal response to your past challenges, your current gratitude, and your expectation of a successful future.

This means you would not merely be *acting as if* you were this bulletproof person – you would actually *become* this bulletproof person.

Most people wait for something to happen outside of themselves to feel good.

They think that once they buy the hot car that they'll feel good about themselves. Or even worse, they think that once they have enough people that are impressed by their hot car, that's when they'll be happy.

Or even worse than that, they think that if they fake who they are on the outside by creating the *Instagrammable* façade of success, that other people will think they are successful, and want to be associated with them.

This entire mindset is built on creating dopamine hits that are manufactured from the outside-in, and is certainly not sustainable.

But if you do the work from the inside-out, you can develop yourself into the person that you truly want to be.

This requires training your brain like a dog.

Your brain will then train your neurological system. Your neurological system will then train your emotions. Your emotions will then train your thoughts. Your thoughts will then train your behavior. Your behavior will then influence your outcome.

This is what I did to spark the beginning of deconstructing my psyche, reprogramming my default emotional loop, and reconstructing myself and my brand.

I literally deconstructed, reconstructed and recalibrated my neurological system, as well as my entire business platform.

This process has produced a level of clarity and certainty within me that has changed my entire outlook on life. This is why I felt so compelled to write this *Second Edition*.

The person I was ten years ago when I wrote the *First Edition* is radically different that the person I am today. I wouldn't say that I changed, but rather evolved and matured.

With maturity comes wisdom, and with wisdom comes the responsibility to share what you have learned with others.

I believe that a leader must continually reinvent themselves. This does not mean that a leader should change with the times, but rather grow as a person as they experience and learn new things. No matter how experienced or wise a leader may be, their journey of learning and developing a deeper understanding of themselves is so important.

The Japanese practice of *Kaizen* is based on the philosophical belief that everything can be improved, and is the commitment to life-long learning and continuous improvement.

This desire to improve is not based on greed, but rather honoring the opportunity to make incremental improvements to one's craft. This is not seen as a chore, but rather an honor.

This deconstruction, reconstruction and recalibration process can be applied to an organization as well as an individual person. In my case, I elected to honor this process and apply it to both.

In this final chapter, I will share with you how I have reinvented *The Darren Sugiyama Companies*, as well as Darren Sugiyama the man.

CHAPTER 11
THE REINVENTION OF THE DARREN SUGIYAMA COMPANIES

If you have already read the *First Edition* of this book, you know that many of my processes and philosophies remain the same.

But as you have also discovered, several chapters from the *First Edition* do not exist in this *Second Edition*.

These chapters were not necessarily *bad* – I just have a different perspective on them today compared to ten years ago.

As I re-read the *First Edition* prior to constructing this *Second Edition*, I noticed a tone of egoism and immaturity that I did not like. Humble-brags, judgements of others and hints of self-righteousness were undertones that came from my ten-years younger self. Some of the attitudes I had about things back then are mildly embarrassing to me today. Hopefully that is a sign of growth.

In this *Second Edition*, I've shared with you many of my successes over the last ten years to illustrate why certain things worked, but I hope my explanations are perceived as *instructional*, not *braggadocios*.

I also hope that my transparency in regards to my mistakes will serve as a *guard rail* for you, for it is easy to veer off the highway and drive off the cliff. My intent is to have you learn from both my past successes and failures, as well as my current successes and recent failures.

Though I am grateful for the lessons I've learned from my past, a big part of my *brand deconstruction* involved letting go of the past – both the successes and the failures – and creating something new from ground zero.

Over the last ten years, I have reinvented and rebranded both my business brand and my personal brand to be more congruent with who I am, what I stand for, and who I truly want to become.

This was a full deconstruction, reconstruction and recalibration of everything I had done up to the point of publishing the *First Edition* of this book.

Anytime you make the commitment to *kill* who you are in order to *give birth* to who you want to become, it requires going backwards initially.

Tiger Woods went through a period during his 2003-2004 seasons where he reconstructed his entire swing with coach Hank Haney. This was the second time Tiger had elected to go through a complete swing overhaul in his career.

People thought it was asinine to change his swing, for he had just won the *Masters* by 12 strokes.

In years just prior to this decision – between 1999 and 2002 – Tiger had won 35% of the *PGA Tour* events and 44% of the *majors* he attended.

ESPN likened Tiger's decision to reinvent his swing to Michelangelo going back and attempting to rechisel a more impressive six-pack on the *Statue of David*.

One golfing coach said, "The only thing Tiger should be changing is this route to the bank."

Every elite golfer constantly tweaks and makes minor mechanical revisions to their swing, but what Tiger Woods did went far beyond that.

This was a conscious decision to undergo a complete overhaul, fundamentally creating an entirely new swing.

Many elite golfers have attempted to do this and failed miserably, deeply regretting their decision in later years.

David Gossett won the *Amateur at Pebble Beach* in 1999 at the tender age of 19. In his rookie season as a professional golfer, he won the *PGA Tour's John Deere Classic*. Despite his overwhelming success, he became convinced that he needed to overhaul his swing. Today, he struggles to break 80.

Craig Perks won the *Players Championship* in 2002, and in 2007, he elected to go through an entire swing overhaul. Perks retired from the game later that year.

The number of golfers who went through complete swing overhauls – in search of the perfect swing – and failed is not small.

Chip Beck, David Duval, Ian Baker-Finch and Seve Ballesteros are just a few of the world's top golfers all fell victim to the full deconstruction/reconstruction of their swings and never recovered.

Tiger Woods' decision to embark on a similar journey through the minefield of a full swing reconstruction was a courageous one.

Kinesiologists and neurologists would explain this process from a mechanical and physiological standpoint as creating a new set of movements, establishing a new *muscle memory*.

But an equally important element of a *total* reconstruction is the mental and emotional aspect, not just the kinesthetic adjustment factors.

Bob Rotella – psychologist to many top professional golfers – says that anytime a golfer embarks on the journey of a full overhaul of their swing, it requires them to go back to square one as a *beginner*.

Making a radical paradigm shift in an already-successful approach can be confusing and emotionally traumatic.

All of a sudden, you are confronted by a conflict between what has already made you successful, and the new ideas that you think might be better.

The first layer of confusion is that there is no absolute certainty regarding which elements should be *kept*, versus which elements should be *replaced*.

The second layer of confusion sparks a litany of variables to consider because it is unclear what new elements should replace the old elements that need to be replaced.

But the third layer of complexity is the most troublesome. There are infinite combinations of these replacement elements combined with the elements that remain. Finding the right combination – where the perfect selection of elements work together in perfect synchronicity – is the *Holy Grail* the perfectionist is in pursuit of.

This perfection is virtually unattainable, but the perfectionist does not waver in their pursuit.

As the perfectionist ventures deep down the dark rabbit hole of exploring this new and unproven way of doing things, they have no idea if their theory is actually going to work.

It is purely based on a hunch.

Statistically speaking, it is very possible that this tireless effort could all be in vain, putting the perfectionist in a worse position than where they originally started.

For Tiger Woods, he would spend the first two years of his swing overhaul going backwards, significantly.

Can you imagine being at the height of dominance on the tour the way Tiger was, and electing to willingly go backwards in pursuit of something even better?

This risk was tremendous.

But Tiger's gamble on himself paid off, as his performance between 2005 and 2008 resulted in him winning 43% of his regular *PGA Tour* events – up from his previous 35% winning percentage.

Anyone that has the brazen courage to dive down this rabbit hole and start digging fervently with *calculated abandon* – not reckless abandon, but *calculated abandon* – is certain to face the severe mental anguish of constantly questioning themselves.

I know this feeling intimately.

I've found myself confused and frustrated during times of recalibration and innovation, with no clarity and no certainty of whether or not my decisions were the right ones.

This is a level of self-inflicted chaos that can literally lead the strongest of warriors to a nervous breakdown and permanent mental illness.

Those that think I am being overly dramatic about this have clearly never gone through this process themselves.

I don't think most people understand just how much of a risk a person incurs by making the decision to go down this road, or how much stress this puts on a person's spirit.

This is not merely *hard work*.

This is *Mission Impossible* and can often times feel like a suicide mission.

It is the decision to bet *all* the marbles on a new unproven idea – an attempt to create something that may not even be possible – where a failure could very easily make a full financial recovery impossible.

In addition, this road is a one-way road, meaning that you cannot easily retrace your steps and easily restore what you once had if the road you picked was the wrong road. You must continue on that one-way road and never attempt to find your way back home through alternate back roads that may or may not exist.

It's like a ship that goes out to sea that cannot find its way back to shore. One could very easily lose themselves in the abyss.

On the surface, it seems like such an unnecessary and risky move by most people's standards, but that's what a perfectionist is willing to endure during their journey from being *great* to becoming a *legend*.

A *full recalibration* of a business model – or a golf swing – means you will go through a period of being *completely uncalibrated*.

The state of being *completely uncalibrated* can only be accurately articulated using a phrase that rhymes with *mucked up*.

It is self-inflicted mental and emotional torture.

But the worst part is, there is no visible light at the end of this tunnel. You have to be willing to make the plunge and risk it all, purely based on a hunch.

As if the mechanics of the recalibration weren't complex enough, in order to get everything to *click*, you need to be *in the zone* mentally and emotionally.

You need to calm your emotions and quiet your mind while standing right in the eye of the storm in order to see things clearly as everything around you appears to be falling apart.

You must become a hybrid between *Godzilla* and *Yoda* – beast and Zen master – to even have a remote chance of making it through the storm.

It is so difficult, it is nearly impossible.

But *nearly impossible* means it *is possible*, and that's what a full overhaul banks on.

This road is not for the weak.

This takes a tremendous amount discipline and emotional strength. It takes a bulletproof mindset and nerves of steel.

I started the recalibration of *DaVinci Financial* in 2016, rolling out my newly created *Employee Retirement Program (ERP)* platform, and let me tell you, it was painfully cumbersome and flopped for almost the entire first year.

Tons of unforeseen challenges punched me dead in the face.

We had to pivot from product to product due to underwriting and processing challenges. We started off with paper applications, group list billing, and employee payroll deductions.

Then we pivoted to an online enrollment platform.

Then we went back to paper applications and used a call center to conduct the health telephone interview because we got the paramed requirements waived.

Then we went to individual billing, premiums paid via ACH, and a completely different technology-driven underwriting process.

It was so frustrating, you have no idea.

Anyone in their right mind would have given up during that first year of reinvention.

But that wasn't the only project I was working on during 2016. I wasn't just recalibrating *DaVinci*.

I was reconstructing my entire platform of companies, which meant an entire deconstruction of everything I had built.

The Deconstruction

Every *reconstruction* requires an initial *deconstruction* first.

As with Tiger's swing, there were some elements worth keeping, some worth destroying, some worth refining, and some new ones that needed to be created from scratch.

It takes a lot of courage to deconstruct, reconstruct, calibrate and recalibrate your entire business.

So there I was in the middle of a complete overhaul – recalibrating one of my companies and starting another one at the same time – and I got hit with a sucker punch that almost knocked me out.

Several of my agents banded together and executed a *coup d'é·tat* against me, stealing the majority of my agency's clients.

I would later find out that they had been planning this for months, plotting against me the entire time, right under my nose.

The financial blow was extremely painful, but I must admit, I was far more hurt emotionally. I had given everything to these people, both personally and professionally. I treated them like family, and when you get betrayed by family, there is no greater pain – like a dagger through the heart.

It is so easy to become bitter and resentful.

You can easily lose your faith in mankind.

When I went through that tumultuous period of mass agent exodus and the stealing of my clients, I knew that going back to my old business model and just rebuilding what I had already built would have been a much easier route than continuing my overhaul.

Inventing and innovating does not produce immediate revenue. It takes time to produce quantifiable results.

I had already proven that my old model was good enough to build a $37 million agency, but deep down in my soul – and I know this might sound ostentatious – I wanted to do bigger things with better people.

I wanted to be aligned with people that shared my vision and lived by my code of honor. The people that left certainly did not embody any of these qualities.

I also wanted to do business with people that I genuinely enjoyed being around.

I once saw an interview with legendary designer Tom Ford, and he said that he only does business with people that he would want to have dinner with at his home, with his family.

As simple as that sounds, that is what I wanted to do too.

So I made the decision to do what Tiger Woods did.

I decided to continue the deconstruction and of my already-proven business model, and pour gasoline on the fire of my full reconstruction, knowing this would send me backwards even further temporarily.

But how far backwards was I willing to go?

One of my favorite movies is *Gattaca* with Uma Thurman, Jude Law and Ethan Hawke.

The movie takes place in a futuristic society where upon birth, a person is biologically tested to determine superiority or inferiority. Ethan Hawke's character is born as an *in-valid* – a genetically inferior human destined for a life of mediocrity.

As a young adult, he purchases the DNA identity of someone born with genetic superiority in order to enroll in the *Gattaca* space program – a program reserved for the genetically elite. With an unbreakable will to succeed, he overcomes all odds despite his genetically inferior DNA.

My favorite scene is where he is put to the test in a challenge to compete in a high-stakes game of *chicken* against a genetically superior person – his brother.

The challenge: To see who could swim the furthest out to sea before turning back to shore.

The two swim far beyond safety until his brother finally gives up and begins to drown. Ethan Hawke's character saves him, dragging him back to shore.

When asked how he was able to achieve everything he had achieved – fooling everyone into believing he was one of the genetically superior few – he replied, "You want to know how I did it? I never saved anything for the swim back."

That's what I decided to do – not save anything for the swim back – and go all-in with my new business model.

The majority of my focus was shifted away from immediate revenue-generating activity towards building this completely new model. This was an agonizing decision because it was in the midst of dealing with the financial aftermath of those agents that left me.

I needed to replace *a lot* of revenue, but I also knew that the right decision was for me to focus on building the new model that would take me to new heights – far beyond what my old model alone could have done – while my immediate revenue suffered.

The Reconstruction

Right in the middle of all of this happening, I launched *Lionsmark Capital* – a life insurance premium financing intermediary firm – with my current business partner, Jeff Faine.

Jeff had a very successful 10-year NFL career and was the highest paid *center* in the league at one time. He had also built a food and hospitality consortium of 29 restaurants and bars back when he was playing in the NFL. Jeff is a beast.

When we first joined forces, we were like Shaq and Kobe, but with Phil Jackson's brainpower downloaded into our frontal lobes.

Our goal was to become the *hired guns* for the top producing life insurance agents and investment advisors in the country, specializing in multi-six-figure and seven-figure premium life insurance policies for the uber-wealthy – a micro-niche in the life insurance industry.

But when you go through a complete deconstruction, reconstruction and recalibration, it takes time to get everything aligned where all pistons are firing, and it always takes longer than you expect.

You have to prepare to go backwards for an undisclosed amount of time, and there is no guarantee that you won't go so far backwards that you drown in the process. This ocean of rough waters has claimed the lives of many.

When I say I went backwards, you have no idea how far backwards I had to go, but I never questioned my decision.

At times, I felt like I was so deep into the abyss, there was no turning back, even if I wanted to.

But that's the key. I never wanted to.

That's what going all-in means.

It is the commitment of not making decisions based on what you see, but rather what you believe in.

I was falling deeper and deeper behind financially, going backwards to the point where I was close to extinguishing all of my financial resources just to stay alive.

But I didn't care. I was fully committed to this decision, and despite what my bank account said, and despite what my CPA told me about my P&L, I believed I was on the right path.

I took myself off payroll but kept paying my employees their full salaries.

I stopped making my mortgage payments, playing a different game of *high-stakes chicken* with the banks in order to refinance my loans.

I was depleting all of my financial reserves and lines of credit, maxing out every credit card I had.

All the while, my wife never complained one bit.

She was committed to this new direction as much as I was.

My days would start at 3:00 A.M. and every day was an exercise in forcing myself to be grateful for the challenges, talking myself into believing that these struggles were making me stronger, not weaker.

I would only spend 10% of my day doing revenue-generating activities, while 90% of my day was spent recalibrating our system.

This was a seemingly illogical thing to do because we desperately needed the revenue, but a disciplined *Thought Leader* must emotionally detach themselves from their immediate needs, and stay focused on building the long-term foundation of their vision.

Every day was an exercise in maintaining this discipline:

1. Meditate on what I'm grateful for.
2. Put on a brave face despite my financial situation.
3. Recalibrate my system in search of a sweet spot that hasn't even been proven to exist yet.
4. Develop a new business model completely different than anything I have ever done before – having the audacity to believe that I could invent something that doesn't exist yet – and take over an industry that has been dominated by the same players for over 20 years.
5. Be sure to fulfill my role as a leader to my people.
6. Be sure to fulfill my role as a leader to my family.
7. Be sure that every move I make honors my new business partner and is not influenced by my then-current financial challenges whatsoever.

I would constantly remind myself that if life is about suffering, and surviving is about finding *meaning* in the suffering, it was imperative that I discover the meaning of this tumultuous time in order to maintain my sanity.

Every day on my drive into the office – when I was all by myself – I would have conversations with God, and every once in a while, I would break down emotionally.

Anger, frustration and rage poured out of my eyes in liquid form. I had so many people counting on me, and I was deathly afraid of letting them down.

Yes, I was afraid.

I had not been afraid of anything for a long time, but my amygdala was sending messages of fear to my entire body.

No alpha male wants to admit this because we are warriors, but I am just being transparent with you. I was definitely afraid.

I never allowed anyone to see me doubt myself or my vision or how much that betrayal hurt me emotionally, but I would slip into a very dark place from time to time.

Resisting the urge to succumb to feelings of bitterness and anger is a discipline. Most of the time I maintained this discipline quite well, but other times, I did not.

If you've ever taken a hit like this, you know this feeling – the feeling of shame that you have fallen to the bottom after you have been at the top for so long.

It is embarrassing thing for an alpha male like me to admit.

But that is the ego talking – false pride – and your ego will always tell you a story that is in opposition to your truth.

That fear generated my fight-or-flight biochemical response, and I chose to use it to my advantage.

I had trained myself through meditation and rewiring my neurological system to change the context of my situation, changing the narrative in my head, which changed my actions.

This is what allowed me to find my truth – the truth of who I was destined to be.

Finding My Truth

It is not an easy road to find your truth, but once you do, you will have a level of clarity that you have never experienced before, and this clarity will give you the unshakeable confidence you need to weather the storm.

As I elaborated on earlier in this book, you must have clarity regarding your *Standard Operating Procedure (SOP)*, but equally as important, you must have ultimate clarity regarding who you are and who you want to be.

The story you tell yourself about who you are is so important. All too often, we allow other people to define who we are and their perceptions about us define our identity.

For so long, my identity was associated with accomplishments.

Mr. exotic car guy.

Mr. $5,000 custom suit guy.

Mr. $37 Million Agency guy.

But when those agents stole much of my agency, I was no longer *Mr. $37 Million Agency guy.*

So if I wasn't that guy anymore, who was I?

In my old office, I had tons of carrier awards hanging on the walls, acknowledging me and my firm for our dominance in the employee benefits industry.

In addition to the awards that hung on my walls, I also had boxes and boxes of awards in storage.

When I moved into my new office space, I literally threw all of them away. I didn't want my identity associated with what I had already accomplished.

The downfall of every successful person begins when they believe in the illusion that they have *made it.*

In my deconstruction process, I decided to approach every day as if it was my first day on the job. I wanted to recapture the same raw grit I had when I was first starting my insurance career, when my tax return showed an annual income of $277. When I punched the proverbial heavy bag, I wanted that *Rocky Balboa snarl* that only someone with nothing to lose has.

Once you're successful, you can only regain this mindset if you are willing to go back to the beginning, cutting ties with your past successes and humbling yourself as a beginner would.

If you're still focused on what you've accomplished in the past, it means you aren't accomplishing much in the present, and I had to prove to myself that I could succeed again from a dead stop.

When I moved into my new office space, the only thing I hung on the wall in my foyer was a painting by a very talented artist and dear friend of mine – Derek Baron – that reads, "Fortune Favors The Bold."

I look at this painting every morning when I arrive at the office, and every evening before I depart.

It reminds me of who I am.

It reminds me of who I want to be: *Bold*.

Being *bold* has nothing to do with what you have accomplished. It has nothing to do with awards hanging on a wall, or the car you drive, or how expensive your watch is.

It has to do with who you truly are.

When your identity is wrapped up in past accomplishments or material items, you are empty inside – void of any value.

However if your identity is defined by who you are inside, if you are full of gratitude, wisdom and courage, you possess the power to move the needle, regardless of the environment.

This is true value, and if you connect with the understanding of why you experience challenges – betrayal, going backwards, and how this ultimately affects your glorious destiny – you can embrace these challenges and be grateful for the outcome they will produce in your life.

I once read something that made it all come together for me:

> *All that can be shaken will be shaken so that what cannot be shaken may remain.*
>
> Hebrews 12:27

This simple principle was the key to my understanding.

Everything I went through was a test to see how much I truly believed in my vision, to see if my vision would be shaken or if it would remain.

It was also a test to see what people in my life would be *shaken* versus who would *remain*.

Those that *remained* would be the ones I was supposed to be aligned with in building what I believed in so strongly.

No other business I have represents this principle more than *Lionsmark Capital*.

I met my current business partner Jeff in 2015. We talked about doing business together from a little over a year, and informally started working together in 2016, codeveloping a premium financing program very different than what the rest of the industry was doing. After a year of development and getting to know each other better, we decided to formally become business partners and together, we started *Lionsmark Capital* in 2017.

When Jeff and I started *Lionsmark*, he lived in Florida and I lived in California. We would start emailing and texting at 4:00 A.M. my time, which was 7:00 A.M. his time, and our days would wrap at 9:00 P.M. my time, which was midnight his time.

We came into the game with a very different approach. We had no interest in being just another premium financing firm. Our vision was to create a brand new model, designed using a completely different paradigm, and to radically change the narrative in the industry.

We set out to be industry disruptors, and I was invigorated about business like never before.

When we first started *Lionsmark*, my other companies were crushing it. But shortly into our newly formed partnership, I experienced the mass exodus of agents that I mentioned earlier.

Jeff was aware of what was happening, but I never shared with him just how much that impacted me from a financial standpoint or an emotional standpoint. I trusted him enough to tell him, but I never wanted him to worry about me or my situation, so I made sure that every decision I made in regards to our partnership was purely based on growth, not based on my financial hardship.

As we got to know each other over the years, we became like brothers. In fact the only thing we've ever argued over was refusing to let each other reimburse the other for expenses. He took care of expenses behind my back, and I took care of expenses behind his back.

We never kept track of any of that. That's what brothers do.

Slowly but surely, we started to gain local traction.

Then we gained regional traction, then national traction.

Before we knew it, we were featured speakers at industry symposiums sponsored by some of the largest insurance carriers and marketing organizations in the country.

In 2019, we were featured speakers at *Peloton's National Symposium*, *FFR's National Symposium*, *Nationwide's Top Producer Symposium*, and several carrier seminars and webinars including *John Hancock, Pacific Life* and *Penn Mutual*.

We had made a name for ourselves in the life insurance industry as premium financiers within the first three years of officially launching and became one of the top players in the country.

Our proprietary premium financing programs were being endorsed and promoted by thirteen major life insurance carriers including *Allianz, Global Atlantic, John Hancock, Nationwide, National Life Group, Pacific Life, Penn Mutual* and several others.

We developed proprietary premium financing programs, including our *Leveraged Index Arbitrage*^{TM} strategy and our *Omakase Pension Alternative*^{TM}, and formed alliances with over a dozen banks, including *U.S. Bank, Wells Fargo, Gracie Point, Cogent Bank, Wintrust, SunTrust,* and several others.

This was the first time in my insurance career where carriers and IMOs were actually referring business to us, and they weren't small deals either.

Six-figure and seven-figure premium life insurance cases were being sent to us as their trusted resource – their hired gun of choice – to be brought in to close the largest deals in the entire life insurance industry.

Our largest death benefit sale at the 3-year mark was $70 million, executed and delivered completely over the phone and via screenshare.

And just as things were really coming together for us, we decided to embark on yet another full recalibration journey – another *Tiger Woods-style* swing overhaul.

We spent the majority of 2019 developing a brand new method of premium financing that we trademarked called the *Omakase Pension Alternative*^{TM}.

We took elements of our *Leveraged Index Arbitrage*™ strategy – our initial proprietary premium financing program that put us on the map – and designed our second proprietary program.

Nothing like this existed in our industry at that time.

Our new program would offer clients with net worth amounts below $5 million something that they never had access to before. *Omakase* would open up an entirely new and untapped market for us – the *HENRY* market (an acronym for *High Earner Not Rich Yet*).

Young physicians, attorneys and other professionals whose incomes were north of $200,000 per year, but whose net worth amounts were below $5 million, could now access our program as an alternative to the outdated pension plan model.

This was a market much different than our standard $25 million+ net worth demographic.

Throughout this reconstruction, I finally got *DaVinci* recalibrated as well.

A big part of *DaVinci's* recalibration was building a proprietary software program that could backtest and stress-test how an Indexed Universal Life insurance policy's cash value growth compares to a qualified retirement account and a managed investment account, using actual backtested historical S&P 500 performance.

To this day, no one else in the life insurance industry has been able to replicate this software.

In the beginning, everyone told me it wouldn't work.

But in 2017 our pilot program was responsible for 25% of all *Pacific Life* life insurance policies sold in Orange County, California… and that was with only three of my agents.

The next year, we implemented our platform with another carrier, and were responsible for 29% of all *Penn Mutual* life insurance policies sold in Orange County in 2018.

The following year in 2019, we were responsible for 38% of all *Penn Mutual* life insurance policies sold in Orange County.

As I write the final chapter of this *Second Edition* in 2020 – right in the middle of this Coronavirus quarantine – *Lionsmark* is forming even more powerful alliances with power players in the industry, as we have just secured relationships with a new team of players including a law firm, a new lender, and a new distribution partner. The team we have assembled and orchestrated will execute a program that this industry has never seen before.

Each day, I let this sink in for a moment and realize that none of this would have been possible had my old model not been shaken, and had I not had the *testicular fortitude* to willingly go through so many deconstructions, reconstructions, and recalibrations.

In addition, none of this would have happened if I was still associated with the people of my past. Though painful at the time, their departure was the best thing that could have happened to me, or rather *for* me.

In the midst of all of this whirlwind of growth, I started another firm – *Worksite MGA* – that offers a brand new employee benefits platform where I provide a proprietary system to group health insurance brokers and voluntary benefits reps to help them double their agency's production.

I have taken my *competitors* and turned them into *partners*, offering them a collaborative partnership opportunity for them to utilize all of my brilliantly curated programs, including:

1. Group Health Insurance
2. Property & Casualty
3. Voluntary Supplemental Insurance
4. Consulting Services for Voluntary Benefits Reps
5. Employee Retirement Program
6. Annuity Rollovers
7. Business Owner Life Insurance for:
    a. Personal Estate Planning
    b. Buy-Sell Agreements
    c. Key-Man Insurance
    d. Non-Qualified Deferred Comp
    e. Financed Pension Alternatives
8. Premium Financing Intermediary Services

This is true leverage – the culmination of over seventeen years of development – with the scale to grow far beyond anything I have ever done.

I don't need to recruit *everybody* because my model maximizes the amount of production per agent. With my new platform, we can produce more premium with less agents, less liabilities and far less headaches.

My entire brand is about clarity, transparency, and collaboration. Gone are the agents with overgrown egos – the wannabe *Dan Bilzerians* and fake *Wolf Of Wall Street* types.

I still use many of the same processes and philosophies in regards to how I interview people and how I communicate our value proposition to our clients, as well as how I position the proprietary nature of our solutions as a career opportunity.

These principles have remained the same, but what has dramatically changed is my brand. The overly flashy, in-your-face images of materialism and egoism are no longer part of my brand.

There's nothing wrong with driving a hot car or owning nice things, but the overt attempt to motivate people through materialism just isn't something I want to be part of anymore.

If this is your brand, please don't take this as a criticism.

I understand that every business is different, and we all have our own preferences regarding the message we choose to put out there. I used to do all of the aspirational brand stuff too, but I made the conscious decision that it is not something I want to be associated with any longer.

Do I drive a *Prius* now? No, I still drive an Italian luxury car.

I haven't exactly downsized my lifestyle in that regard, but the difference is, I don't flash my lifestyle in people's faces or promote it on social media anymore.

The fact is, most people don't even know what I drive now.

The flashy aspirational brand I used to promote so heavily has been replaced by an understated brand that purely focuses on delivering revolutionary and superior performance for our clients.

My new brand can be summed up in two words:

1. Authenticity.
2. Transparency.

Gone are the flashy images I used to promote on social media like the one below.

Back then, I thought a flashy brand was required to grab people's interest through material intoxication. But when I started seeing other people promoting a similar *look-at-me* type of brand, it was kind of like looking in the mirror, and I didn't like what I saw.

If I value my family, my friendships, my integrity and living a life of gratitude, why didn't my social media posts reflect this?

As I said earlier in this book, when you put out *shit*, you attract the *flies*. The flies lay eggs, and eventually the maggots hatch.

This is what prompted the reconstruction of my brand – killing the old in order to give birth to the new.

The only car I've posted on social media since this radical transformation is my *weekend beater vehicle* – a 1984 Jeep CJ-7.

It has soft half-doors, a bikini top, and is a 4-speed, clunky stick shift. It's loud, beat up and a ton of fun.

My 10-year old son absolutely loves cruising with me in this Jeep. In fact, he likes it better than any of my previous flashy cars because my Jeep is about enjoying the experience, not the acknowledgement and the adulation of others.

It's not expensive or luxurious.

The only reason it ended up on social media is because it's an integral part of activities I do with my son. We take it to the beach, fishing, and just cruising around running errands in.

It's not about image. It's about enjoying time with my son.

Most of the images I post on social media today are with my family like the one below.

Perhaps one day I'll trade in my proclivity towards luxury cars and just drive a Jeep as my daily driver. In fact maybe I'll do it just to prove I don't need trophy cars anymore.

I'm not quite there yet. ☺

We are all works in progress, and we all have our own path to follow. I just encourage you to find your own path and not fall victim to trying to impress everyone else.

The biggest person you need to impress is yourself.

My Radical Shift In Mindset Over The Last 10 Years

As for my reputation in the industry, everyone who needs to know my level of success already knows it.

For those that don't know, perhaps it's better for them to not know. If they knew, it wouldn't help the growth of my business anyway, and it might actually breed jealousy and contempt.

My old ego wanted everyone to know how successful I was. But today, the only thing I want everyone to know is that I am an honorable person, that my ability to execute is unparalleled, and that I am a man of my word.

My current brand is solely about performance – transparently showing our clients that our strategies are indisputably superior – and that our client outcomes are unrivaled.

Monetary success usually comes with this level of performance, but our entire focus is on our value proposition, not our commission checks.

This is also the focus of my message in the recruiting process.

I'm looking for agents that want to be part of my culture of excellence, not a culture of monetary success.

These are the *right* agents for my firm.

I encourage you to recruit the *right* agents, not the *most* agents. That being said, the *right* agents for your firm might be a different demographic than the *right* agents for mine.

This is something you need to define for yourself, for we all have our own preferences.

Now, you may be saying to yourself, "Why not do both?"

Perhaps the right business model for you is to mass recruit, mass train, build a 100+ agent army, and get the most out of everyone possible.

You can certainly to do that.

You also might be saying, "I worked hard for my Ferrari and I like driving it… and I'm not giving up my diamond encrusted *Breitling* watch or my closets full of *Louis Vuitton* either… and I don't care if people find my *in-your-face* flashiness offensive!"

Hey, there's nothing wrong with all of that either assuming that is your style and brand preference. In fact, if you like that image, I hope you make so much money that you can go out and buy two of every luxury item your heart desires.

There's nothing wrong with liking what you like, so please don't misunderstand what I'm saying.

Just make sure that it makes *you* happy.

Don't do it to impress and motivate others.

It will attract the wrong people to your firm and it will backfire on you one day.

There is obviously more than one *right* way to build an insurance empire, no doubt about it. I am just sharing with you my own personal business model transformation.

You need to *do you*. Just make sure it is the *authentic you*, not a *fabricated you* that you think you have to be for other people.

Struggle Is A Stage, Not An Outcome

If you are currently going through challenges in your business, I encourage you to look at your current situation not as an indication of your future success, but rather as a necessary stage of your business *story arc*.

In a movie or television series, the *story arc* is defined as the episodic nature of the story unfolding over time. Each episode is but a chapter of many chapters within the full story.

The arc is made up of many peaks, plateaus, and valleys; each necessary components in telling an intriguing story – a story worth telling and a story worth listening to.

Similarly, a *narrative arc* describes the full progression of the story. A great storyline usually follows this *narrative arc* format:

1. The beginning environment appears to be peaceful.
2. A potential tension is detected.
3. The seed of conflict is identified.
4. The conflict intensifies and grows exponentially to a peak.
5. The conflict is resolved.

Often times, we feel that whatever progression we have experienced in our lives thus far will continue in a linear fashion.

If things have not gone well, we assume things will either stay the same or progressively get worse.

If things have gone exceedingly well for us, we assume things will either continue to go well, or progressively get better.

Neither are necessarily true.

Things can change on a dime for the better, or for the worse.

The key is to acknowledge that life is filled with peaks, plateaus and valleys. None of them are permanent, and none of them are indicative of what is next to come.

Most importantly, none of them define who you are or who you are destined to become.

Your current situation is but a mere chapter in your *story arc*.

We all have a different *story arc* with a different sequence of chapters and number of chapters.

The key is to be grateful for each chapter – even the rough ones where conflict peaks – because each chapter is a necessary component of your story.

If you are full of gratitude inside, no matter what happens externally, you will be able to come out of any storm because you have trained your mental, emotional and biochemical state to be that of a champion.

If you find yourself in challenging times right now, just remember that struggle is a stage you're going through, not your final outcome.

How My Struggles Have Become Blessings

The situation I find myself in today is definitely not normal, but it has become my *new normal*, and all things considered to be *normal* can easily be taken for granted.

This is why I believe it is so important to take an inventory of all the things in your life that you are grateful for. It is so easy to take your *new normal* for granted, regardless of how blessed your *new normal* is.

I make it a practice to remind myself of what life could be like if my blessings were taken away from me, and more importantly, what less fortunate people's *current normal* must feel like.

My worst day could very easily be someone else's best day.

I have also learned to be grateful for challenges and setbacks, for they have made me a better human being.

They have made me more resilient, stronger and wiser.

They have tested the strength of my marriage, and my wife and I are now closer and stronger than ever.

They have afforded me the platform to talk to my son about challenges and how to deal with them, not just from a philosophical standpoint, but from a practical and personal standpoint. When he goes through challenges himself, he will know he is not alone in this human experience, and he will be better equipped to deal with them because I will have trained him how.

Equally as important, I have learned to be humble in the midst of success, for I realize that I am not 100% responsible for any of my blessings. I have been afforded opportunities and have been blessed with unlikely relationships that have opened doors for me, and it doesn't make me any less of a man to have walked through such doors.

No one does it entirely on their own.

There is no such thing as 100% self-made.

I have learned the importance of being willing to go backwards in order to take quantum leaps forward. There is no shame in going backwards despite how the optics may appear from the outside looking in.

People love it when it appears that *The Mighty* have fallen, but the truly mighty know they have not *fallen*. They have willingly gone backwards in preparation to take quantum leaps forward.

But I didn't want to be considered one of *The Mighty*.

I wanted to be considered one of *The Bold*.

The Bold are willing to swim deep into the abyss – saving nothing for the swim back – because they have no interest in swimming back. *The Bold* have committed to swimming to the other side in search of the new land they believe exists.

The Bold do not rely on the temporary feeling of happiness in order to feel good about themselves, hence they are not affected by their circumstances, for that is what common men do.

What drives *The Bold* is the confidence they have created for themselves from within.

The Bold do not seek *happiness*. Instead, they seek adventure and in the process create their own *joy*.

The Difference Between Happiness & Joy

The biggest lesson I've learned over the last ten years is that all the accomplishments in the world will never give you *true joy*.

True joy is only attained when we are grateful for three things:

1. What we've been through.
2. Who we have become.
3. Who we have the potential to be.

This is the difference between *happiness* and *joy*.

Happiness is due to our circumstances, and is temporary. It feels good in the moment, but needs to be replaced by another experience that is even better than the last. Over time, it becomes harder and harder to experience happiness because your *new normal* no longer feels special.

This is the problem with pursuing happiness.

Joy on the other hand is due to our understanding of what is truly important, and is permanent. It has very little to do with external experiences. It is a constant state of being that comes from knowing who you are and being comfortable and confident in your own skin. Joy is impervious to challenges because it embraces conflict, for it knows that from conflict comes growth and invaluable lessons about who you are and who you want to become.

This is the value of understanding the difference between *happiness* and *joy*. Once you are able to accept and embrace this, you become less interested in trying to create the optics of success because you know you are already on the right path, and you are secure in who you are and what you stand for.

You become less interested in acquiring *stuff*, because you already have what's important. You become less bothered by other people's false criticisms of you, because those whose opinions matter already know who you are inside.

The imperfections that come with authenticity become more and more beautiful to you, because you understand the *valleys* of life are what makes your story more compelling, not the *peaks*.

The Ultimate Irony Of Gratitude

What I am about to tell you is without a shadow of doubt the most important lesson to take away from this book.

Everything I have shared with you over the last 11½ chapters hits the crescendo right here, right now – the secret of all secrets.

I have talked extensively about removing the *want* from your consciousness, and perhaps you're thinking to yourself, "How can I achieve more if I want less? Isn't that the opposite of motivation?"

This is the greatest misconception of motivation, drive and passion. When you are driven to accomplish more because you are discontent with your current situation, you are operating from a position *lack*.

You *want* more because you feel you do not *have* enough.

Translation: You feel that *you* are not enough.

But when you feel complete – when you have true joy inside your heart – you operate from a position of strength because you aren't desperately chasing an outcome. You don't want or need an outcome to make you feel good because you already feel good inside. Your emotions are not dictated by your external environment, but rather by your intentionally produced biochemistry.

This enables you to operate with an intention of *giving* instead of *taking*. You have no need to take because you know you already have everything that's important. You have no reservation of giving because you know how much you have, and the well of true joy which you draw from is bottomless.

You also don't need the acceptance of others because you already have certainty about who you are.

Because you do not lack, you exude a positive aura. Your positive expectations have been produced by creating the thoughts that create your body's surge in production of oxytocin.

You also feel worthy to receive because you feel you have already received so much – the definition of gratitude.

As a result of feeling worthy of receiving, you receive even more, all the while focusing on giving, not receiving.

The same thing that happens when a woman sees a man that doesn't need attention.

She is drawn to him like a magnet – like a vortex.

The less attention he needs, the more female attention he receives. There is an magnetic energy a man exudes when he is the opposite of desperate. He doesn't *want* because he already *has* everything he needs inside.

This is the power of being a *giver* instead of a *taker*.

The giver isn't focused on *wanting out of lack*.

They are focused on *giving out of abundance*.

You see, the grand irony of ridding yourself of *want* is that opportunities begin to fall into your lap without you chasing them because the universe recognizes the magnetism of true joy.

Alliances form with the right people without you hunting them down. Coincidental events happen to your advantage without you forcing them, but there is nothing coincidental about them.

Because you are full of gratitude, you become a vortex that draws great people and great opportunities towards you.

Your work ethic must look like you believe it is entirely up to you to manifest your success, but as you engage in your daily practice of gratitude recognition, you will become a magnet – a vortex.

Do not misinterpret what I'm saying here.

You cannot merely think positive thoughts and have success fall into your lap. That's nonsense.

You must work as if you are carrying the entire world on your shoulders, not saving anything for the swim back.

You must create content, products and platforms as if you were trying to win a *Nobel Prize*.

But if you can master the practice of gratitude recognition and be disciplined enough to practice it on a daily basis, you will be able overcome yourself... and if you can overcome yourself and your ego, you can overcome anything this world throws at you.

You will become an unstoppable warrior.

The weapons may form against you, but they will never prosper, because you have learned how to achieve true joy from within through gratitude.

I closed the *First Edition* of this book by saying, "The greatest pleasure life is accomplishing things that other people said you could not do."

Although these types of accomplishments are very satisfying, this pleasure only lasts for a moment. What you accomplish is never as important as who you become in the process.

So let me revise the closing of this *Second Edition* – ten years later and ten years wiser – from a new perspective.

> "The greatest pleasure in life is realizing how blessed we truly are – being grateful for good times and bad times – knowing that our accomplishments are never as important as our gratitude. This is true joy."
>
> -Darren Sugiyama

ABOUT THE AUTHOR

Darren Sugiyama is a grateful husband, father, author, businessman, and motivational speaker. He currently lives in Orange County, California with wife and son.

WWW.DARRENSUGIYAMA.COM

www.ingramcontent.com/pod-product-compliance
Lightning Source LLC
Chambersburg PA
CBHW071659170426
43195CB00039B/2320